Learning Unreal Engine Game Development

A step-by-step guide that paves the way for developing fantastic games with Unreal Engine 4

Joanna Lee

PUBLISHING

BIRMINGHAM - MUMBAI

D1297031

Learning Unreal Engine Game Development

First published: February 2016

Production reference: 1240216

Published by Packt Publishing Ltd.
Livery Place
35 Livery Street
Birmingham B3 2PB, UK.

ISBN 978-1-78439-815-6

www.packtpub.com

Credits

Author
Joanna Lee

Reviewers
Michele Bertolini

Kyle Langley

Daniel Jonathan Valik

Commissioning Editor
Edward Bowkett

Acquisition Editor
Subho Gupta

Content Development Editor
Preeti Singh

Technical Editor
Ankita Thakur

Copy Editor
Sonia Cheema

Project Coordinator
Shweta H. Birwatkar

Proofreader
Safis Editing

Indexer
Tejal Daruwale Soni

Production Coordinator
Nilesh Mohite

Cover Work
Nilesh Mohite

About the Author

Joanna Lee has more than 8 years of experience in game development. She has designed and programmed various video games. She first started working with Unreal's game engine in 2005 and is very excited to be able to author a book about the newest Unreal Engine 4. She has also worked with many other engines as well as reviewed books and videos on Cry Engine 4.

I would like to thank my parents and sister for their constant support in my game development journey and my brother, Jerome, who first drew me into the world of gaming. I also want to thank all my ex-colleagues and managers for their patience while teaching me about developing games and making each work day a pleasure.

Lastly, I would also like to thank the amazing team at Packt Publishing for guiding me through the publishing process and making this book possible.

About the Reviewers

Michele "Budello" Bertolini always had a passion for videogames, but his way into the industry had been long and strange. In his youth, he was more interested in becoming a professional volleyball player despite studying computer science and computer graphics.

Then, he stopped growing and he only had one choice left.

Michele's education and background are strongly technical due to his master's in computer engineering degree. Through the course of his career, he's developed various artistic skills, passing drawing and photography courses. He's also a keen observer of nature. He thinks of himself as a technical guy with a good taste.

34BigThings is a small indie company based in Turin, Italy. Currently, it's involved in two titles: Redout, a tribute to old racing monsters, such as F-Zero, WipeOut, Rollcage, and POD and Hyperdrive Massacre, an 80s inspired multiplayer fragfest for up to four local players, which is focused on kinesthetic, tactical, and shooting skills.

> I'd like to thank all the guys and gals in 34BigThings: first friends, then coworkers.

Kyle Langley is a self-taught game designer currently working for Vex Studios. He has also worked with Emotional Robots Inc, Sony Online Entertainment, and High Moon Studios. He is the author of *Learn Programming With Unreal Script*, which is aimed at teaching beginners the concept of object-oriented programming as well as the initial aspects of programming for the Unreal Development Kit. He was also the technical reviewer of *Source SDK Game Development Essentials, Packt Publishing*. You can find more about him on his website (www.dotvawxgames.com).

Daniel Jonathan Valik is an industry expert in the areas of Unified/Universal Communications, IaaS, SaaS, DevOps, Cloud Native Apps, WebRTC, Cloud Voice and Business Voice, mobile computing, social networking and UC-enabled Contact Center technologies. Daniel has driven these topics for more than 15 years in the IT and telecommunication industries, and he has also lived and worked in different regions, such as Europe, Southeast Asia, and the United States. Daniel is currently a senior technical product marketing manager for Cloud Native Apps, DevOps and Cloud Technologies at the VMWare HQ in Palo Alto, California. He was previously the senior technical product marketing manager for the Skype Developer Platform and Skype for Business Online at the Skype/Microsoft HQ in Redmond, Washington, USA. As part of the Skype product team, Daniel drove the positioning of Skype for Business, Online, Developer Platform, a UC-enabled contact center, and other emerging technologies. He holds a number of technical certifications, including Microsoft Certified Trainer; he has a double master's degree (MBA), a master's degree (MAS) in general business, and additionally holds a degree in international business management.

www.PacktPub.com

Support files, eBooks, discount offers, and more

For support files and downloads related to your book, please visit www.PacktPub.com.

Did you know that Packt offers eBook versions of every book published, with PDF and ePub files available? You can upgrade to the eBook version at www.PacktPub.com and as a print book customer, you are entitled to a discount on the eBook copy. Get in touch with us at service@packtpub.com for more details.

At www.PacktPub.com, you can also read a collection of free technical articles, sign up for a range of free newsletters and receive exclusive discounts and offers on Packt books and eBooks.

https://www2.packtpub.com/books/subscription/packtlib

Do you need instant solutions to your IT questions? PacktLib is Packt's online digital book library. Here, you can search, access, and read Packt's entire library of books.

Why subscribe?

- Fully searchable across every book published by Packt
- Copy and paste, print, and bookmark content
- On demand and accessible via a web browser

Free access for Packt account holders

If you have an account with Packt at www.PacktPub.com, you can use this to access PacktLib today and view 9 entirely free books. Simply use your login credentials for immediate access.

Table of Contents

Preface

Many people know what a game is, and a lot of people play games every day. But how many people know how to create a game? Game development using Unreal Engine 4 allows aspiring game creators to develop professional-looking games quickly. Unreal Engine 4 provides very polished game development tools and capabilities that allow vast amounts of customization for almost any game that you can dream of.

What this book covers

Chapter 1, An Overview of Unreal Engine, covers introductory content about what a game engine is, specifically for Unreal Engine 4 and its history. You will get an overview of the features of Unreal Engine 4 and how it can help you to create a game.

Chapter 2, Creating Your First Level, explains how to create your first room using the Box Brush, add materials to texture the walls/floor, and learn how to place static objects to enhance the look of the room.

Chapter 3, Game Objects – More and Move, covers the structure of a simple object type, known as Static Mesh, and how objects in Unreal interact with one another. This chapter also introduces Blueprints, which is the graphical scripting of Unreal Engine 4.

Chapter 4, Material and Light, shows you how to customize your level in greater detail by learning how to create your own basic custom Material and how to use simple lights to light up the interior of the level.

Chapter 5, Animation and AI, covers how animation works in Unreal Engine and how to implement simple AI in your game level.

Chapter 6, A Particle System and Sound, explains how to add visual and sound effects to your level.

Chapter 7, Terrain and Cinematics, shows you how to add the final touches to your level using terrain manipulation and cinematics.

What you need for this book

You will need to create a free account with Epic Games to start using Unreal Engine 4.

Who this book is for

This book is meant for those of you who are new to game development and want to learn how games are created.

Conventions

In this book, you will find a number of text styles that distinguish between different kinds of information. Here are some examples of these styles and an explanation of their meaning.

Code words in text, database table names, folder names, filenames, file extensions, pathnames, dummy URLs, user input, and Twitter handles are shown as follows: "In my case, it will be `Chapter2Level`."

New terms and **important words** are shown in bold. Words that you see on the screen, for example, in menus or dialog boxes, appear in the text like this: "The **Modes** window gives you the power to create and place objects into the game world."

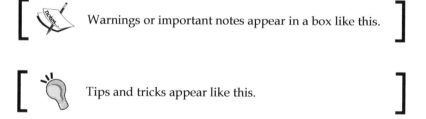

Warnings or important notes appear in a box like this.

Tips and tricks appear like this.

Reader feedback

Feedback from our readers is always welcome. Let us know what you think about this book—what you liked or disliked. Reader feedback is important for us as it helps us develop titles that you will really get the most out of.

To send us general feedback, simply e-mail feedback@packtpub.com, and mention the book's title in the subject of your message.

If there is a topic that you have expertise in and you are interested in either writing or contributing to a book, see our author guide at www.packtpub.com/authors.

Customer support

Now that you are the proud owner of a Packt book, we have a number of things to help you to get the most from your purchase.

Downloading the example code

You can download the example code files from your account at http://www.packtpub.com for all the Packt Publishing books you have purchased. If you purchased this book elsewhere, you can visit http://www.packtpub.com/support and register to have the files e-mailed directly to you.

Downloading the color images of this book

We also provide you with a PDF file that has color images of the screenshots/ diagrams used in this book. The color images will help you better understand the changes in the output. You can download this file from: http://www.packtpub.com/ sites/default/files/downloads/LearningUnrealEngineGameDevelopment_ ColorImages.pdf.

Errata

Although we have taken every care to ensure the accuracy of our content, mistakes do happen. If you find a mistake in one of our books—maybe a mistake in the text or the code—we would be grateful if you could report this to us. By doing so, you can save other readers from frustration and help us improve subsequent versions of this book. If you find any errata, please report them by visiting http://www.packtpub.com/submit-errata, selecting your book, clicking on the **Errata Submission Form** link, and entering the details of your errata. Once your errata are verified, your submission will be accepted and the errata will be uploaded to our website or added to any list of existing errata under the Errata section of that title.

To view the previously submitted errata, go to https://www.packtpub.com/books/content/support and enter the name of the book in the search field. The required information will appear under the **Errata** section.

Piracy

Piracy of copyrighted material on the Internet is an ongoing problem across all media. At Packt, we take the protection of our copyright and licenses very seriously. If you come across any illegal copies of our works in any form on the Internet, please provide us with the location address or website name immediately so that we can pursue a remedy.

Please contact us at copyright@packtpub.com with a link to the suspected pirated material.

We appreciate your help in protecting our authors and our ability to bring you valuable content.

Questions

If you have a problem with any aspect of this book, you can contact us at questions@packtpub.com, and we will do our best to address the problem.

1
An Overview of Unreal Engine

First of all, thank you for picking up this book. I am sure you are excited to learn how to make your own game. In this chapter, I will run you through the different fundamental components in a game and what Unreal Engine 4 offers to help you make your dream game.

The following topics will be covered in this chapter:

- What is in a game?
- The history of **Unreal Engine (UE)**
- How is game development done?
- The components of UE and its editors

What goes into a game?

When you play a game, you probably are able to identify what needs to go into a game. In a simple PC shooting game example, when you press the left mouse button, the gun triggers. You see bullets flying, hear the sound of the gun and look around to see if you have shot anything. If you did hit something, for example, a wall, the target receives some form of damage.

As a game creator, we need to learn breakdown what we see in a game to figure out what we need for a game. A simple breakdown without going into too much detail: link the mouse click to the firing of the bullets, play a sound file that sounds like a gun firing, display sparks (termed as **particle effect**) near the barrel of the gun and the target shows some visible damage.

Bearing this example in mind, try visualizing and breaking any game down into its fundamental components. This will greatly help you in designing and creating a game level.

There is a lot going on behind the scenes when you are playing a game. With the help of Unreal Engine, the interaction of the many components has been designed and you will need to customize it for your own game. This is a huge time saver when you use an engine to create a game.

What is a game engine?

What a game engine does is that it provides you with tools and programs to help you customize and build a game; it gives you a head-start in making your own game. Unreal Engine is one of the more popular choices in the market currently and it is free for anyone to use for development (royalties need to be paid only if your game makes a profit; visit https://www.unrealengine.com/custom-licensing for more information). Its popularity is mainly due to its extensive customizability, multiplatform capabilities, and the ability to create high quality AAA games with it. If you intend to start a career in game development, this is definitely one of the engines you want to start playing with and using to build your portfolio.

The history of Unreal Engine

Before explaining what this amazingly powerful game engine can do and how it works, let us take a short trip back into the past to see how UE came about and how it has evolved into what we have today.

For gamers, you are probably familiar with the Unreal game series. Do you know how the first Unreal game was made? The engineers at Epic Games built an engine to help them create the very first Unreal game. Over the years, with the development of each generation the Unreal game series, more and more functionalities were added to the engine to aid in the development of the game. This, in turn, increased UE's capabilities and improved the game engine very quickly over the years.

In 1998, the first version of UE made the modding of a first player shooting game possible. You could replace Unreal content using your own and tweak the behavior of the **non-player characters** (**NPCs**), also known as **bots** (players that are controlled by the computer through artificial intelligence) using UnrealScript. Then multiplayer online features were added into UE through the development of *Unreal Tournament*, which is an online game. This game also added PlayStation 2 to the list of compatible platforms in addition to the PC and Mac.

By 2002, UE had improved by leaps and bounds, bringing it into the next generation with the development of a particle system (a system to generate effects such as fog and smoke), static mesh tools (tools to manipulate objects), a physics engine (allows interaction between objects such as collisions) and a Matinee (a tool to create cut scenes, which is a brief, non interactive movie). This improvement saw to the development of the *Unreal Championship* and *Unreal Tournament 2003*. The release of *Unreal Championship* also added the Xbox game console to the list, with multiplayer capabilities in Xbox Live.

The development of Epic's next game *Unreal II: The Awakening* edged UE forward with an animation system and overall improvement with their existing engine. The development of faster Internet speeds in the early 2000s also increased the demand of multiplayer online gaming. *Unreal Tournament 2004* allowed players to engage in online battles with one another. This saw the creation of vehicles and large battlefields, plus improvements in online network capabilities. In 2005, the release of *Unreal Champion 2* on the Xbox game console reinforced UE capabilities on the Xbox console. It also saw the creation of a very important feature of a new third-person camera. This opened up greater possibilities in the types of games that could be created using the engine.

Gears of War, one of the most well-known franchises in the video games industry, pushed Epic Games to create and release the third version of its game engine, *Unreal Engine 3*, in 2006.

The improvement of the graphics engine used DirectX 9/10 to allow more realistic characters and objects to be made. The introduction of **Kismet**, which is a visual scripting system, allowed game and level designers to create game play logic for more engaging combat play without having to delve into writing codes. Platform capabilities of UE3 include Xbox360 and PlayStation 3 was added. There was a revamp in the light control and materials. UE3 also had a new physics engine. *Gears of War 2* released in 2008 saw the progressive improvements to UE3. In 2013, the *Gears of War Judgment* was released.

PC online gaming was also under the radar of Epic Game's developers. In 2009, Atlas Technology was released to be used in conjunction with UE to allow **massively multiplayer online games (MMOG)** to be created.

The increasing demand of mobile gaming also led to UE3 being pushed in the direction of increasing its supportability for various mobile platforms. All these advancements and technological capabilities have made UE3 the most popular version of Unreal Engine and it is still very widely used today.

UE3 dominated the market for 8 years until UE4 came along. UE4 was launched in 2014 and introduced the biggest change by replacing Kismet with the new concept of **Blueprint**. We will discuss more about the features of UE4 later in the chapter.

Game development

Each game studio has its own set of processes to ensure the successful launch of its game. Game production typically goes through several stages before a game is launched. In general, there is a preproduction/planning, production stage, and postproduction stage. Most of the time is normally spent in the production stage.

Game development is an iterative process. The birth of an idea is the start of this process. The idea of the game must first be tested to see if it is actually fun to the target audience. This is done through prototyping the level quickly. Iterations of this prototype into a fully-fledged game can go from weeks to months to years.

The development team takes care of this iteration process. Everyone's contribution of the game throughout the development cycle directly affects the game and its success.

Development teams loosely consist of several specialized groups: artists (2D/3D modeler, animator), cinematic creators, sound designers, game designers, and programmers.

Artists

They create all visible objects in the game from menu buttons to the trees in the game level. Some artists specialize in 3D modeling, while others are focused on animation. Artists make the game look beautiful and realistic. Artists have to learn how to import their created images/models, which are normally created first using other software such as 3DMax, Maya, and MODO into UE4. They would most likely need to make use of Blueprint to create certain custom behaviors for the game.

Cinematic creators

Many cinematic experts are also trained artists. They have a special eye and creative skills to create short movie scenes/cut scenes. The Matinee tool in UE4 will be what they would be using most of the time.

Sound designers

Sound designers have an acute sense of hearing and they are mostly musically trained. They work in the sound labs to create custom sounds/music for the game. They are in charge of importing sound files into UE4 to be played at suitable instances in the game. When using UE4, they would be spending most of their time using the Sound Cue Editor.

Game designers

Designers determine what happens in the game, what goes on in the game, and what the game will be about. In the planning stage, most of the time will be spent in discussion, presentations, and documentation. In the production stage, they will oversee the game prototyping process to ensure that the game level is created as designed. Very often designers spend their time in the Unreal Editor to customize and fine-tune the level.

Programmers

They are the group that looks into the technology and software the team needs to create the game. In pre-production, they are responsible for deciding which software programs are required and are capable of creating the game. They also have to ensure that the different software used are compatible with one another. Programmers also write codes to make the objects created by the artist come alive according to the idea that the designers came up with. They program the rules and functionality of the game. Some programmers are also involved in creating tools and research for the games. They are not directly involved in creating the game but instead are supporting the production pipeline. Games with extreme graphics usually have a team of researchers optimizing the graphics and creating more realistic graphics for the game. They spend most of their time in codes, probably coding in Visual Studio using C++. They are also able to modify and extend the features of UE4 to support the needs of the game that they are developing.

The components of Unreal Engine 4

Unreal Engine is a game engine that helps you make games. Unreal Engine is made up of several components that work together to drive the game. Its massive system of tools and editors allows you to organize your assets and manipulate them to create the gameplay for your game.

Unreal Engine components include a sound engine, physics engine, graphics engine, input and the Gameplay framework, and an online module.

The sound engine

The sound engine is responsible for having music and sounds in the game. Its integration into Unreal allows you to play various sound files to set the mood and add realism to the game. There are many uses for sounds in the game. Ambient sounds are constantly in the background. Sound effects can be repeated when needed or one-off and are triggered by specific events in the game.

In a forest setting, you can have a combination of bird sounds, wind, trees, and leaves rustling as the ambient sound. These individual sounds can be combined as a forest ambient sound and be constantly playing softly in the background when the game character is in the forest. Recurring sounds such as footprint sound files can be connected to the animation of the walking movement. One-time sound effects, such as the explosion of a particular building in the city, can be linked to an event trigger in the game. In Unreal, the triggering of the sounds is implemented through cues known as **Sound Cue**.

The physics engine

In the real world, objects are governed by the laws of physics. Objects collide and are set in motion according to Newton's laws of motion. Attraction between objects also obeys the law of gravity and Einstein's theory of general relativity. In the game world, for objects to react similarly to real life, it has to have the same system built through programming. Unreal physics engine makes use of the PhysX engine, developed by NVIDIA, to perform calculations for lifelike physical interactions, such as collisions and fluid dynamics. The presence of this advanced physics engine in place allows us to concentrate on making the game instead of spending time making objects interact with the game world correctly.

The graphics engine

For an image to show up on screen, it has to be rendered onto your display monitor (such as your PC/TV or mobile devices) The graphics engine is responsible for the output on your display by taking in information about the entire scene such as color, texture, geometry, the shadow of an individual object and lighting, and the viewpoint of a scene, and consider the cross-interaction of the factors that affect the overall color, light, shadow, and occlusion of the objects.

The graphics engine then undergoes massive calculations in the background using all these information before it is able to output the final pixel information to the screen. The power of a graphics engine affects how realistic your scene will look. Unreal graphics engine has the capabilities to output photorealistic qualities for your game. Its ability to optimize the scene and to process huge amount calculations for real-time lighting allows users to create realistic objects in the game.

This engine can be used to create games for all platforms (PC, Xbox, PlayStation, and mobile devices). It supports DirectX 11/12, OpenGL, and JavaScript/WebGL rendering.

Input and the Gameplay framework

Unreal Engine consists of an input system that converts key and button presses by the player into actions performed by the in-game character. This input system can be configured through the Gameplay framework. The Gameplay framework contains the functionality to track game progress and control the rules of the game. **Heads-up displays (HUDs)/user interfaces (UIs)** are part of the Gameplay framework to provide feedback to the player during the course of the game. Gameplay classes such as GameMode, GameState, and PlayerState set the rules and control the state of the game. The in-game characters are controlled either by players (using the PlayerController class) or AI (using AIController class). In-game characters, whether controlled by the player or AI, are part of a base class known as the **Pawn** class. The **Character** class is a subset of the **Pawn** class, which is specifically made for vertically-oriented player representation, for example, a human.

With the Unreal Gameplay framework and controllers in place, it allows for full customization of the player's behavior and flexibility, as shown in the following figure:

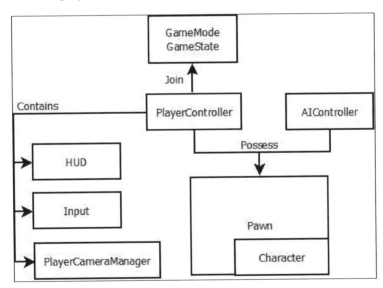

Light and shadow

Light is a powerful tool in game creation. It can be used in many ways, such as to create the mood of a scene or focus a player's attention on objects in the game. Unreal Engine 4 provides a set of basic lights that could be easily placed in your game level. They are **Directional Light**, **Point Light**, **Spot Light**, and **Sky Light**.

Directional Light emits beams of parallel lights, Point Light emits light like a light bulb (from a single point radially outward in all directions), Spot Light emits light in a conical shape outwards, and Sky Light mimics light from the sky downwards on the objects in the level:

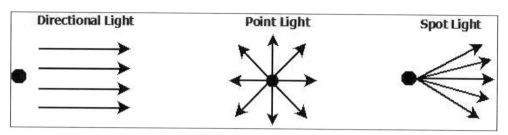

The effective design of light also creates realistic shadows for your game. By choosing the types of light in the level, you can affect both the mood and time it takes to render the scene, which in turns affect the frames per second of your game. In the game world, you can have two types of shadows: static and dynamic. Static shadows can be prebaked into the scene and, which makes them quick to render. Dynamic shadows are changed during runtime and are more expensive to render. We will learn more about lights and shadows in *Chapter 4, Light and Environment Control.*

Post-process effects

Post-process effects are effects that are added at the end to improve the quality of the scene. Unreal Engine 4 provides a very good selection of post-process effects, which you can add to your level to accentuate the overall scene.

It offers full scene **high dynamic range rendering (HDRR)**. This allows objects that are bright to be very bright and dark to be very dark, but we are still able to see details in them. (This is NVDIA's motivation for HDR rendering.)

UE4 post-process effects include Anti-Aliasing using **Temporal Anti-Aliasing (TXAA)**, Bloom, Color Grading, Depth of Field, Eye Adaptation, Lens Flare, Post Process Materials, Scene Fringe, Screen Space Reflection, and Vignette. Although a game is often designed with the post-process effects in mind, users are normally given the option to turn them off, if desired. This is because they often consume reasonable amount of additional resources in return for better visuals.

Artificial intelligence

If you are totally new to the concept of **artificial intelligence (AI)**, it can be thought of as intelligence created by humans to mimic real life. Humans created AI to give objects a brain, the ability to think, and make decisions on their own.

Fundamentally, AI is made up of complex rule sets that help objects make decisions and perform their designed function/behavior. In games, NPCs are given some form of AI so that players can interact with them. For example, give NPCs the ability to find a sweet spot to attack. If being attacked, they will run, hide, and find a better position to fight back.

Unreal Engine 4 provides a good basic AI and lays the foundation for you to customize and improve the AI of the NPCs in your game. More details on how AI is designed in Unreal Engine will be discussed in *Chapter 5, Animation and AI*.

Online and multiplatform capabilities

Unreal Engine 4 offers the ability to create game for many platforms. If you create a game using Unreal Engine 4, it is portable into different platforms, such as Web, iOS, Linux, Windows, and Android. Also, **Universal Windows Platform (UWP)** will soon be added as well. It also has an online subsystem to provide games the ability to integrate functionalities that are available on Xbox Live, Facebook, Steam, and so on.

Unreal Engine and its powerful editors

After learning about the different components of Unreal Engine, it is time to learn more about the various editors and how they are able to empower us with the actual functionalities to create a game.

Unreal Editor

Unreal Engine has a number of editors that help in the creation of the game. By default, the Unreal Editor is the startup editor for Unreal Engine. It can be considered as the main editor that allows access to other subsystems, such as the Material and Blueprint subsystems.

The Unreal Editor provides a visual interface made up of viewports and windows to enable you to import, organize, edit, and add behaviors/interactions to your game assets. Other subeditors/subsystems have very specialized functions that allow you to control details of an asset (how it looks, how it behaves).

The Unreal Editor, together with all the subsystems, is a great tool especially for designers. It allows physical placement of assets and gives users the ability to control gameplay variables without having to make changes in the code.

Material Editor

Shaders and Materials give objects its unique color and texture. Unreal Engine 4 makes use of physically-based shading. This new material pipeline gives artists greater control over the look and feel of an object. Physically-based shading has a more detailed relationship of light and its surface. This theory binds two physical attributes (micro surface detail and reflectivity) to achieve the final look of the object.

In the past, much of the final look is achieved by tweaking values in the shader/material algorithms. In Unreal Engine 4, we are now able to achieve high quality content by adjusting the values of the light and shading algorithms, which produces more consistent and predictable results. More details about Shaders and Materials will be provided in *Chapter 4, Light and Environment Control*. The following screenshot shows the Material Editor in UE4:

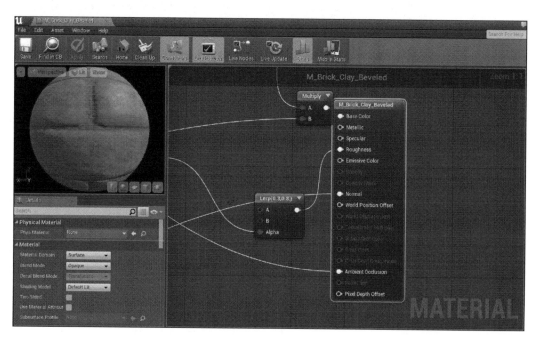

The Cascade particle system

The Cascade particle system provides extensive capabilities to design and create particle effects. Effects from things such as smoke, sparks, and fire can be created by designing the size, color, and texture of each particle and how groups of these particles interact with each other to mimic real-life particle effect behavior. The following screenshot shows the Cascade particle system in UE4:

The Persona skeletal mesh animation

The Persona animation system lets you design and control the animation of the skeleton, skeleton mesh, and sockets of a character. This tool can be used to preview a character's animation and set up blend animation between key frames. The physics and collision properties can also be adjusted through **Physics Asset Tool (PhAT)**. The following screenshot shows the Persona animation system in UE4:

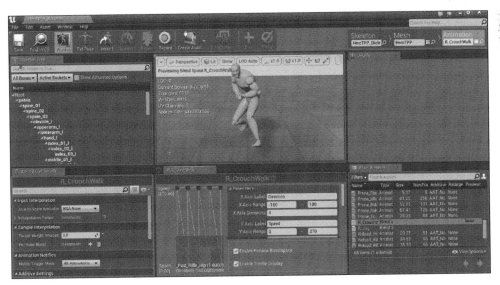

Landscape – building large outdoor worlds and foliage

To create large outdoor spaces using the editor, Unreal Engine provides sculpting and painting tools through the Landscape system to help us with it. An efficient **level of detail (LOD)** system and memory utilization allows large scaled terrain shaping. There is also a Foliage editor to apply grass, snow, and sand into the outdoor environment.

Sound Cue Editor

The control of sound and music is done via the Sound Cue Editor. Sounds and music are triggered to play via cues known as **Sound Cues**. The ability to start/stop/repeat/fade in or out can be achieved using this editor. The following screenshot shows the Sound Cue Editor in UE4:

Matinee Editor

The Matinee Editor toolset enables the creation of game cut scenes and movies. These short clips created could be used to introduce the start of a game level, tell a story before the game begins or even as a promotional video for the game. The following screenshot shows the Matinee Editor in UE4:

The Blueprint visual scripting system

The Blueprint system is a new feature in Unreal Engine. Unreal Engine 4 is the first engine to utilize this revolutionary system. For those who are familiar with Unreal Engine 3, it can be thought of as the enhanced and improved combined version of the Unreal scripting system, Kismet, and the Prefab functionality. The Blueprint visual scripting system enables you to extend code functionality using visual scripting language (box-like flow diagrams joined with lines). This capability means that you do not have to write or compile code in order to create, arrange, and customize behavior/interaction of in-game objects. This also provides nonprogrammers (artists/designers) with the ability to prototype or create a level quickly and manipulate gameplay without having to tackle the challenges of game programming. A cool feature of Blueprint is that you can create variables like in programming by clicking on the object and selecting **Create Variable**. This opens up what developers can do without messing around with complex coding.

To help developers debug Blueprint scripting logic, you can see the sequence of events and property values visually on the flow diagrams as it is being executed. Similar to troubleshooting in coding, break points can also be set to pause a Blueprint sequence. The following screenshot shows the Level Blueprint Editor in UE4:

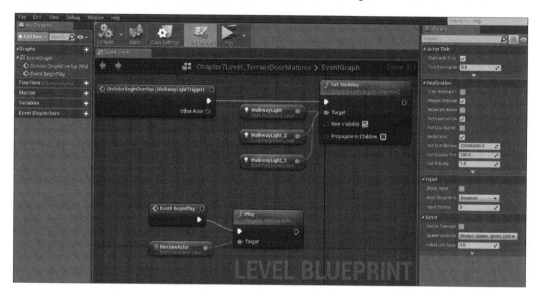

Unreal programming

The access to Unreal Engine's source code gives users the freedom to create almost about anything they can dream of. Functionalities of the base code can be extended and customized to create whatever the game needs to have. Learning how Unreal Engine works from the inside can unlock its full potential in game creation.

Unreal Engine has also incorporated very useful debugging features for the coding folks. One of them is the **Hot Reload** function. This tool enables changes in the C++ code to be reflected immediately in the game. To facilitate quick changes in code, Unreal Engine has also included **Code View**. By clicking on a function of an object in the **Code View** category, it shows you directly the relevant codes in Visual Studio where you could make code changes to the object.

Versioning and source control can be set up for game projects that include code changes.

Unreal objects

Actors are the base class of all gameplay objects in Unreal. For the Actors to have more properties and functionalities, the Actor class is extended to various more complex classes. In terms of programming, the Actor class acts as a container class to hold specialized objects called Components. The combination of the functionalities of the Components gives the Actor its unique properties.

A beginner's guide to the Unreal Editor

This is a quick overview of what we can do with the Unreal Editor. We will briefly touch on how we can use the various windows in the editor to create a game.

The start menu

When starting up Unreal Engine, you will be first brought to a menu window by default. This new start menu is simple and easy to navigate. It features a large tab that allows you to select which version of game engine you want to launch and has a clear representation of the projects you have created. It also provides access to Marketplace, which is a library of game samples that are created by others, which you could download (some free, some paid). The menu also provides latest updates and news from Epic to ensure developers are kept abreast of the latest development and changes. The following screenshot shows the start menu:

Project Browser

After launching the desired version of Unreal Engine, the Unreal Project Browser pops up. This browser provides you with the option to create game levels that have been pre-customized. This means that you have a list of generic levels, which you can start building your game levels with. For those who are new to game making, this feature lets you dive straight into building various types of games quickly. You can have a first-person shooting level and third-person game setup, or a 2D/3D side-scrolling platform level directly in either **Blueprint** or **C++** as the base template. What is so awesome about the **New Project** tab is that it also allows you to select your target device (PC/mobile), image quality target, with or without the Unreal content included in the startup project. The following screenshot shows the Project Browser:

Content Browser

When the Unreal Editor starts, there is a default layout of various windows and panels. One of them is the **Content Browser**. The **Content Browser** is a window where you can find all the content (game assets) that you have. It categorizes your assets into different folders such as Audio, Materials, Animations, Particle Effects, and so on. This window has also the **Import** button, which lets you bring in game assets that were created using other software into the game. The following screenshot shows the default location of the **Content Browser** (outlined in green):

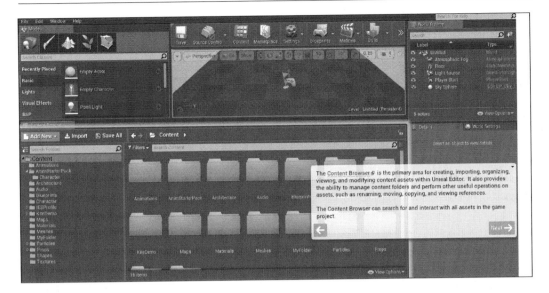

Toolbar

The **Toolbar** is a customizable ribbon that provides quick access to tools and editors. The default layout includes quick access to the Blueprint and Matinee editors. Quick play and launch game function is also part of the standard ribbon layout. These buttons allow you to quickly view your creation in-game. The following screenshot shows the default **Toolbar**:

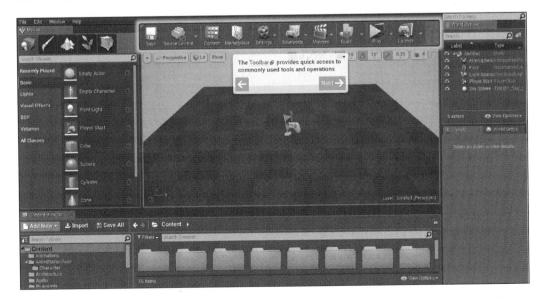

Viewport

The **Viewport** is the window to the game world so what you see is what is in the game. If you have created a level using one of the options provided in the **New Project** menu, you would notice that the camera has been adjusted accordingly to the settings of that pre-customized level. This is the window that you will use to place objects into and move them around. When you click on the **Play** button in the toolbar, this **Viewport** window comes alive and allows you to interact with game level. The following screenshot shows the **Viewport** window being highlighted in the editor:

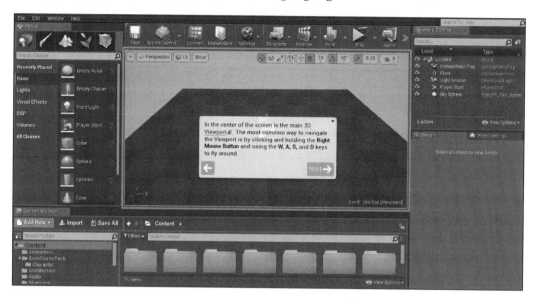

Scene Outliner

The **Scene Outliner** contains the list of objects that are placed in the scene. It is only what is loaded currently in the scene. You can create folders and have customized names for the objects (to help you identify the objects easily). It is also a quick way to group items so that you can select them and make changes in bulk. The following screenshot shows the **Scene Outliner** highlighted in the editor:

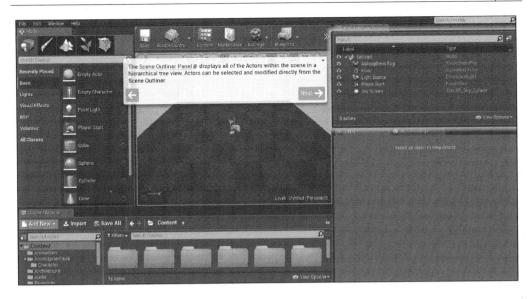

Modes

The **Modes** window gives you the power to create and place objects into the game world. You can select the type of activity you wish to execute. Select from Place, Paint, Landscape, Foliage and Geometry Editing. Place is to put objects into the game world. Paint allows you to paint vertices and textures of objects. Landscape and Foliage are useful tools for making large scale natural terrains in the game. Geometry Editing provides the tools to modify and edit the object. The highlighted area in the following screenshot shows the **Modes** window:

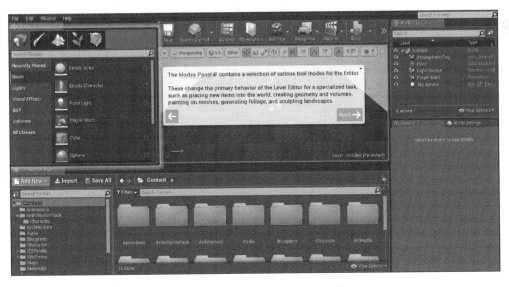

Summary

In this chapter, we covered introductory content about what a game engine is, specifically Unreal Engine 4 and its history. We also talked a little about how games are developed and various roles that exist in a game company to help create different components of a game. Then, we covered the different components of Unreal Engine and how we can use these different features to help us make our game. Lastly, we covered the different editors that are available to us to help us customize each of the components of the game.

In the upcoming chapters, we'll be going into the details of the functionalities and features of Unreal Engine 4. In the next chapter, you will be exposed to some basic functions in the Unreal Editor and start making your own game level.

2
Creating Your First Level

In this chapter, you will create and run a simple level with the help of step-by-step instructions. Since the objective of this book is to equip you with the skills to confidently create your own game using Unreal Engine 4 and not to simply follow a list of steps to create a fixed example, I will provide as much additional information as possible that you could use to create your own game level as we go about learning the basic techniques.

In this chapter, we will cover the following topics:

- How to control views and viewports

- How to move, scale, and rotate objects in a level

- How to use the BSP Box brush to create the ground and a wall using the **Additive** mode

- How to carve a hole in a wall using the **Subtractive** mode of the BSP Box brush

- How to add a simple **Directional Light** to a level to mimic sunlight

- How to spawn a player who's facing the right direction on a map using **Player Start**

- How to create the sky in your map using atmospheric fog

- How to save the map you've created and set it as the default load up map for a project

- How to add a material to the geometries you've created so that it looks realistic

- How to duplicate BSP Brushes to help create things quickly

- How to add props (which are also known as **static meshes**) to a room

- How to concentrate light on important parts of a map using **Lightmass Importance Volume**

Exploring preconfigured levels

Before we create a level, it is good to have an idea of what levels look like in Unreal Engine 4. Unreal Engine 4 offers the possibility to load up various types of game levels with a default playable level that's straight from the **Project Browser** menu option (this pops up immediately after launching the Unreal Editor). Personally, I really like this particular new feature of Unreal Engine 4 as it gives me a quick feel of the types of presets that are available, and I could easily select something as a base for the game level I want to create.

We will create a new map using one of the preset project types as the base for our first level.

How to quickly explore different project types

I normally click on the **Play** button on the toolbar after a project loads with the default level. The play function allows you to be in a game and you can see what has been precreated for you in the level.

Creating a new project

In this chapter, we will use the **Blueprint First Person** template to create our first game project.

The steps to create a new **Blueprint First Person Project** are as follows:

1. Launch Unreal Engine 4.
2. Select the **New Project** tab.
3. Select **Blueprint** and then **First Person**.
4. Choose a name and path for the project (or leave it as the default MyProject).
5. Click on **Create Project**.

Ensure that the **With Starter Content** option is selected.

On creation of the project, the default example level for Blueprint First Person will load. The following screenshot shows how the default level looks:

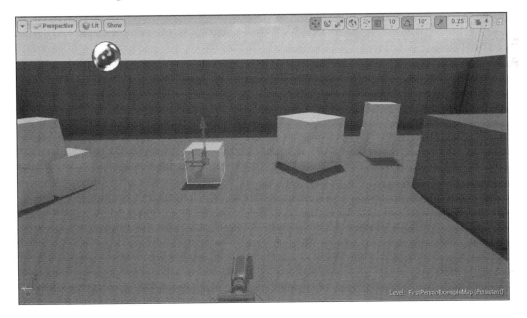

Using the preset project type with the example level, the first thing you'll probably want to do is run the level and see what the default game level contains.

Navigating the viewport

Using the loaded example level, you should get yourself familiarized with the mouse and keyboard controls in order to navigate in the viewport. You might consider bookmarking this section until you can navigate the viewport to zoom in/out or view any object from all angles easily.

Views

Here is some quick information on the different views in 3D modeling creation: the example map is loaded by default in the **Perspective** view. Other than having the map in the **Perspective** view, you can change what you see in the viewport in the top, side, or front views, respectively. The option to switch to any of these is in the left-hand corner of the viewport. The following screenshot shows the location of the button to press so that you can switch views:

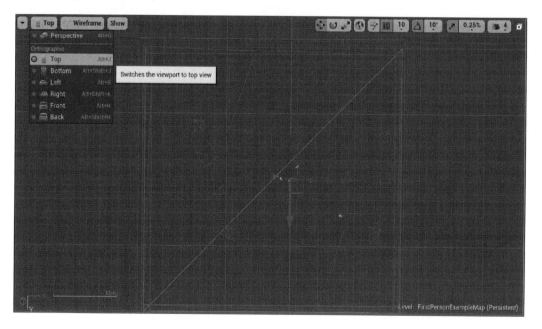

If you wish to see more than one view concurrently, navigate to **Windows | Viewports** and then select any of the viewports (The default viewport uses **Viewport 1**.).

The selected viewport number will pop up. You can drag and dock this **Viewport** window and add it to the default **Viewport 1**. The following screenshot shows **Viewport 1** and **Viewport 2** displayed at the same time (one in the **Perspective** view and the other in the **Top** view):

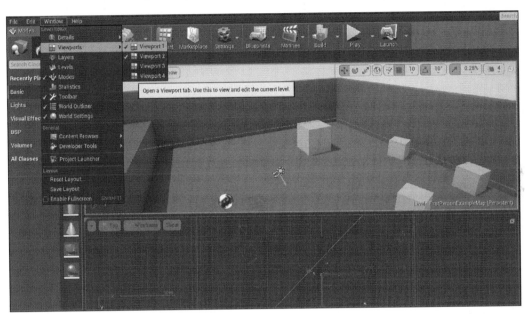

Control keys

Here are some of the key presses to help you move around and view objects:

In the **Perspective** view:

Shortcut action	Description
Left-click + drag	This moves the camera forward and backward and rotates from left to right
Right-click + drag	This rotates the viewport camera
Left-click + right-click + drag	This moves objects up and down

In the **Orthographic (Top, Front,** and **Side)** view:

Shortcut	Description
Left-click + drag	This creates a marquee selection box
Right-click + drag	This pans the viewport camera
Left-click + right-click + drag	This zooms the viewport camera in and out

For those of you who are familiar with games, you can use WASD to navigate the camera in the editor too.

WASD control in the **Perspective** view:

Shortcut action	Description
Any mouse click + *W*	This moves the camera forward
Any mouse click + *A*	This moves the camera to the left
Any mouse click + *S*	This moves the camera backward
Any mouse click + *D*	This moves the camera to the right

On selection of an object:

Shortcut action	Description
W	This displays the **Translation** tool
E	This displays the **Rotation** tool
R	This displays the **Scale** tool
F	This focuses the camera on a selected object
Alt + *Shift* + Drag along the $x/y/z$ axis	This duplicates an object and moves it along the $x/y/z$ axis

Creating a level from a new blank map

Now that you are familiar with the controls, you are ready to create a map on your own. In this chapter, we will go through how to build a basic room from scratch. To create a new map for your first person game, go to **File | New Level…**. The following screenshot shows you how to create a new level:

There are two options when creating a new level: **Default** and **Empty Level**. Select **Empty Level** to create a completely blank map. The following screenshot shows you the options that are available when creating a new level:

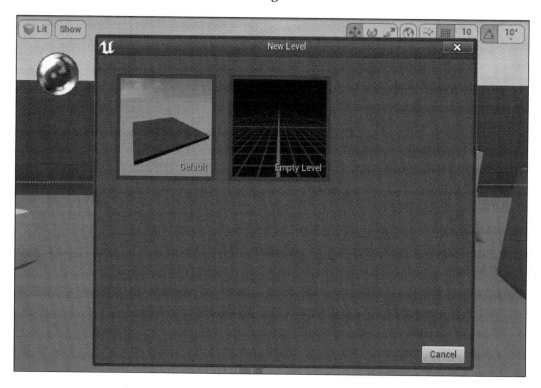

Do not be surprised when the viewport is void. We will add objects to the level in the next few sections. The following screenshot shows what an empty level looks like in the **Perspective** view:

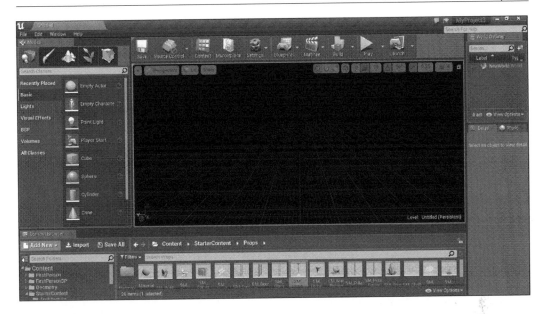

Creating the ground using the BSP Box brush

The BSP Box brush can be used to create rectangular objects in the map. The first thing to do when creating a level is to have a ground to stand on.

Before we begin with this, make sure the viewport is in the **Perspective** view. We will mainly use this view for most of the level creation unless specified explicitly.

Go to the **Modes** window, click on **BSP** and then click and drag **Box** into the viewport. This is where you can find the Box brush:

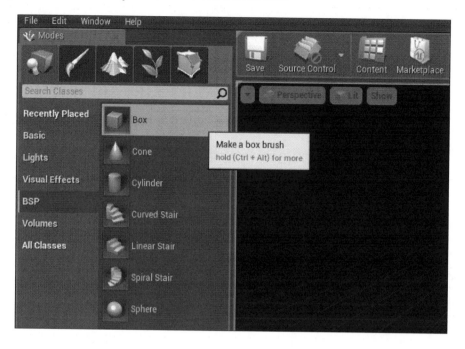

Here, a Box brush has been successfully added to the viewport:

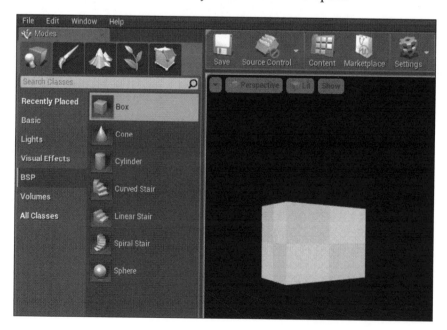

You have now successfully created your first object in the level. We will go on to change the size of this box to a suitable size so that it can act as the ground for the level.

Select the box that was just created, and go to **Details | Brush Settings**. Fill in the following values for **X**, **Y**, and **Z**. The following screenshot shows the values that need to be set:

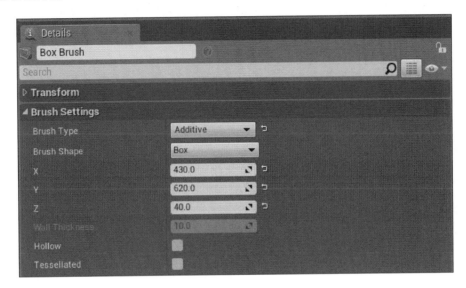

When you have set the values correctly, the box should look like this:

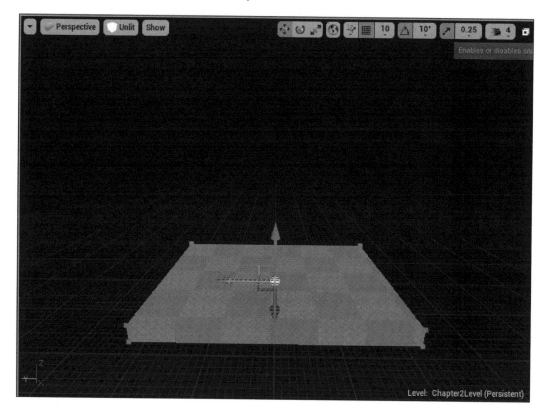

Useful tip – selecting an object easily

To help you select objects in the level more easily, you can go to **World Outliner** (its default location is in the top right-hand corner of the editor), and you will see a full list of all the objects in the level. Click on the name of an object to select it and its details will also be displayed. This is a very useful way to help you select objects when you have many objects in the level. The following screenshot shows how **World Outliner** can be used to select the Box brush (which we've just created) in the level:

Useful tip – changing View Mode to aid visuals

If you have difficulties seeing the box, you can change **View Mode** to **Unlit** (the button is in the viewport that's next to the **Perspective** button). The following screenshot shows you how to change **View Mode** to **Unlit**:

Adding light to a level

To help us see the level better, it is time to learn how to illuminate the level. To mimic ambient light from the sun, we will use **Directional Light** for the level.

In the same way as adding a BSP Box brush, we will go to **Modes Window | Lights | Directional Light**. Click and drag **Directional Light** into the **Viewport** window. The following screenshot zooms in on the **Modes** window, showing that the **Directional Light** item can be created by dragging it into the viewport:

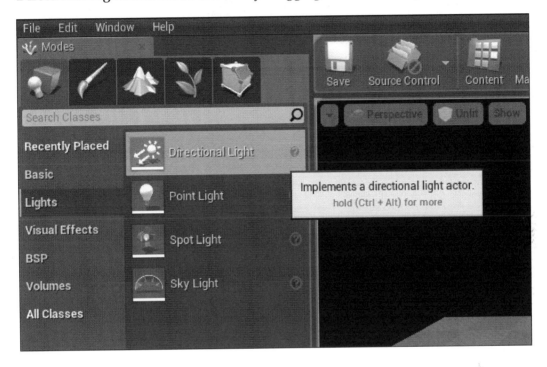

For now, let's place the light just slightly above the BSP Box brush as shown in the following screenshot:

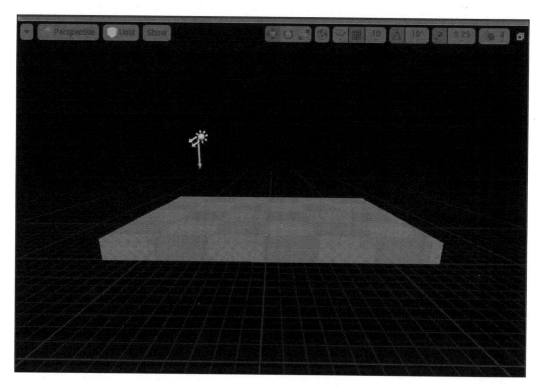

Useful tip – positioning objects in a level

To position an object in a level, we use the **Transform** tool to move objects in the x, y, and z directions. Select the object and press the *W* key to display the **Transform** tool. Three arrows will appear to extrude from the object. Click and hold the red arrow to move the object along the *x* axis, the green arrow to move it along the *y* axis, and the blue arrow to it move along the *z* axis.

To help you position the objects more accurately, you can also switch to the **Top** view when moving objects in the x and y directions, the **Side** view for adjustments in the y and z directions, and the **Front** view to adjust the x and z directions.

For those of you who want precise position control, you can use **Details**. Select the object to display details. Go to **Transform | Location**. You can select **Relative** or **World position** by clicking on the arrow next to **Location**. Change the **X**, **Y**, and **Z** values to move the object with more precision.

Adding the sky to a level

After the addition of light to the level, we will proceed to add the sky to the level. Click on **Modes | Visual | Atmospheric Fog**. In a similar way to adding light and adding a Box BSP, click, hold, and drag this into the viewport. We are almost ready to take a first look at what we have just created. Hang in there.

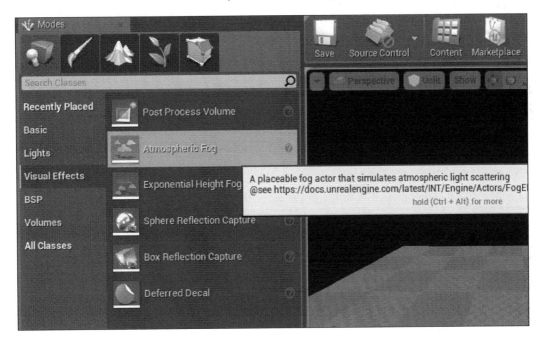

Adding Player Start

For every game, you need to set where the player will spawn. Go to **Modes | Basic | Player Start**. Click, hold, and drag **Player Start** into the viewport.

This screenshot shows the **Modes** window with **Player Start**:

Place **Player Start** in the center of the ground or slightly above it as shown in the following screenshot:

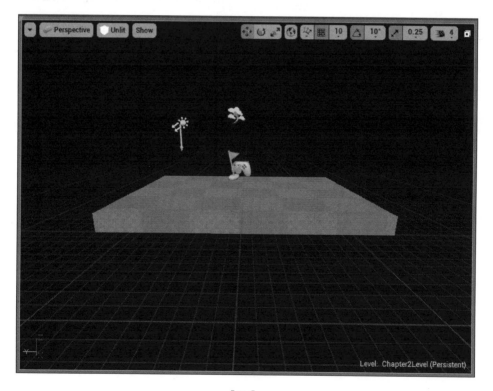

Deselect `Player Start` by pressing the *Esc* key. The light blue arrow from `Player Start` indicates the direction in which the player will spawn the game starts. To adjust the direction that the player faces upon spawning, rotate `Player Start` until the light blue arrow points in this direction. Take a look at the following tip on how to rotate an object.

Useful tip – rotating objects in a level

To rotate an object in a level, we use the **Rotate** tool to rotate objects around the x (row), y (pitch), and z (yaw) directions. Select the object and press the *E* key to display the **Rotate** tool. Three lines with a box tip will appear to extrude from the object. Click and hold the red arrow to rotate the object around the x axis, the green arrow to rotate it around the y axis, and the blue arrow to rotate it around the z axis.

Another way to rotate an object more accurately is by controlling its rotation through the actual rotation values found under **Details**. (Select the object to be rotated to display its details). In the **Transform** tab, go to **Rotation**, and set the **X**, **Y**, and **Z** values to rotate the object. There is an arrow next to **Rotation** that you can click on to select if you want to adjust the rotation values for **Relative** or **World**. When you select to rotate an object using the **Relative** setting, the object will rotate relative to its current position. When the object is rotated using the **World** setting, it will be relative to the world's position.

If you want the player controller (as shown in the preceding screenshot) to have the light blue arrow facing inwards and away from you, you will need to rotate the player controller 180 degrees around the *y* axis. Enter **Y** as 180 under the **Relative** setting. The player controller will be rotated in the manner shown in this screenshot:

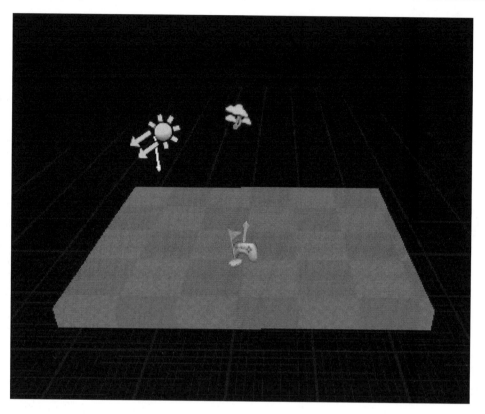

Viewing a level that's been created

We are now ready to view the simple level that we have just created.

Before viewing the level, click on the **Build** button, as shown in the following screenshot, to build the light, materials, and so on, needed for this level. This step ensures that light is properly rendered in the level.

After building the level, click on the **Play** button, as shown in this screenshot, to view the level:

The following screenshot shows how the level looks. Move the mouse up, down, left, and right to see the level. Use *W*, *A*, *S*, and *D* to move the character around the level. To return to the editor, press *ESC*.

Saving a level

Navigate to **File** | **Save As...** and give the map you have just created a name. In our example here, I have saved it as Chapter2Level in the .../UnrealProjects/ MyProject/Content/Maps path, where MyProject is the name of the project.

Configuring a map as a start level

After saving your new map, you may want to also set this project to load this map as the default map. You can have several maps linked to this project and load them at specific points in the game. For now, we want to replace the current Example_Map with the newly created map that we have. To do so, go to **Edit | Project Settings**. This opens up a page with configurable values for the project. Go to **Game | Maps & Modes**. Refer to the following screenshot to take a look at how **Maps & Modes** is selected.

Look under **Default Maps** and change both **Game Default Map** and **Editor Default Map** in the map that you have just saved. In my case, it will be Chapter2Level. Then, close the project settings. When you start the editor and run the game the next time, your new map will be loaded by default.

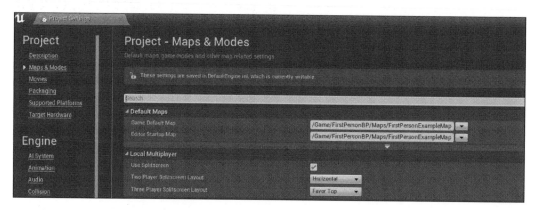

Adding material to the ground

Now that we have created the ground, let us make the ground look more realistic by applying a material to it.

Go to **Content Browser | Content | StarterContent | Materials**. Type wood into the **Filters** box. The following screenshot shows the walnut polished material that we want to use for the ground's material:

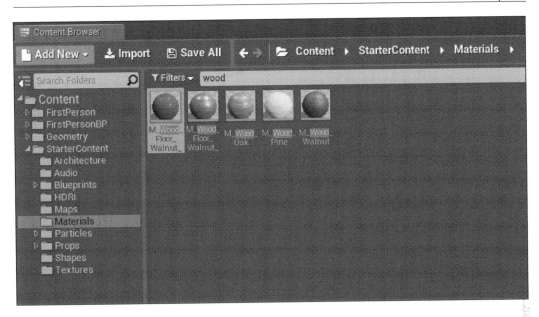

Click, hold, and drag **M_Wood_Floor_Walnut_Polished** into the viewport area and drop it on the top surface of the ground. The resulting effect should look like this:

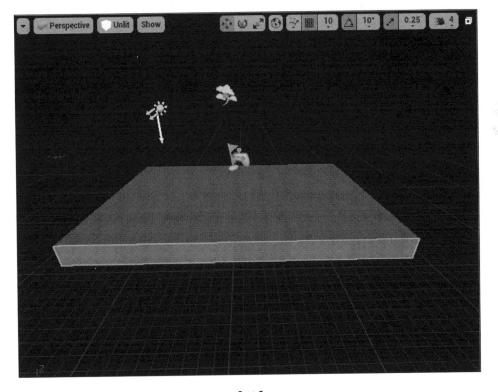

Adding a wall

Now we are ready to add walls to prevent the player from falling off the map. To create walls, we will use the same BSP Box brush to create a wall. As we have just added a material in the previous step, you will need to clear this material selection by clicking on anything in **Content Browser**. This will prevent new geometries from being created using the same material.

Similar to creating the ground, go to **Modes | BSP | Box**. Click, hold, and drag into the viewport. Set the dimensions of the BSP box as X = 30, Y = 620, and Z = 280. To help us view and position the wall, use the controls to rotate the viewport. You can also use the different views to help position the wall onto the ground. Here, you can see how the wall should be positioned (note that I have panned the camera to view the level from a different angle):

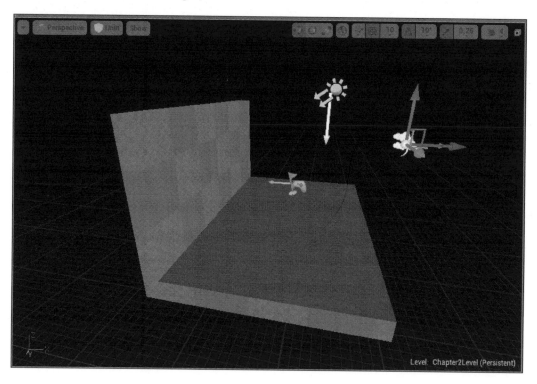

Duplicating a wall

Now duplicate the wall by first selecting the wall created in the earlier step. Make sure the **Transform** tool is displayed (if not, press *W* once when object is selected).

Click and hold one of the axes (the *x* axis, in the preceding example case) while holding down *Alt + Shift* as you drag the current wall in the x direction. You would notice that there is another copy of the wall moving in this direction. Release the keys when the wall is in the right position. Use normal translation controls to position the wall as shown here:

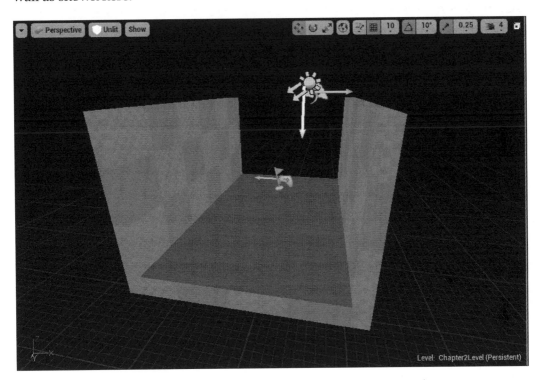

Creating an opening for a door

The room is now almost complete. We will learn how to carve into a BSP Box brush to create an opening for a door.

Drag a new BSP Box brush into the map: X = 370, Y = 30, and Z = 280. Position this wall to seal one side of the room as shown in the following screenshot:

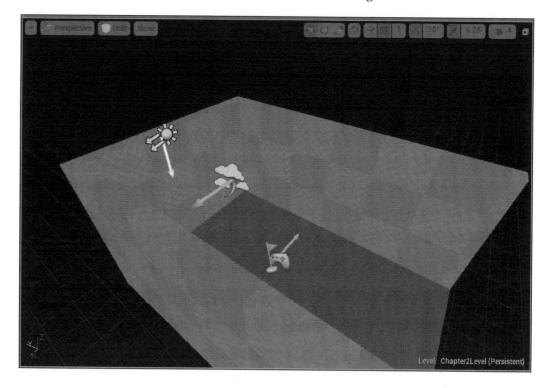

Till now, we have been using the **Additive** mode (add the radio button that is selected) to create a BSP Box brush. To create an opening in the wall, we will create another BSP Box brush using the **Subtractive** mode. Ensure that you have selected it as shown in the following screenshot. Drag and drop the BSP Box brush in the same manner as before into the viewport. As for the dimensions of this brush, we will approximate it to the size of the door, where X = 115, Y = 30, and Z = 212.

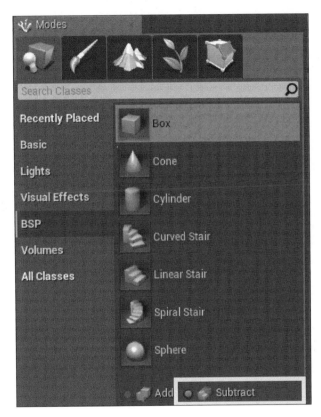

When the **Subtractive** BSP Box brush is positioned correctly, it will look something like this:

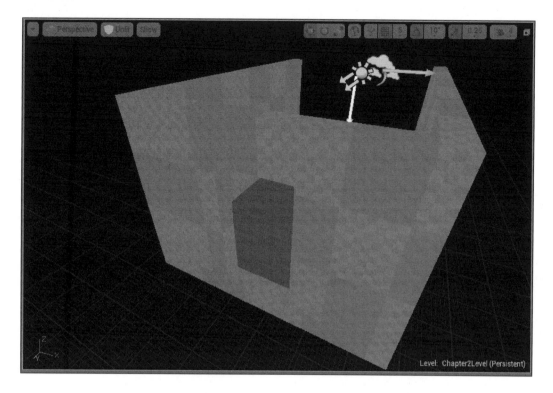

To help you position the **Subtractive** BSP Box brush, you can switch to the **Front** view to place the door more or less in the center. The following screenshot shows the **Front** view with the **Subtractive** BSP Box brush selected:

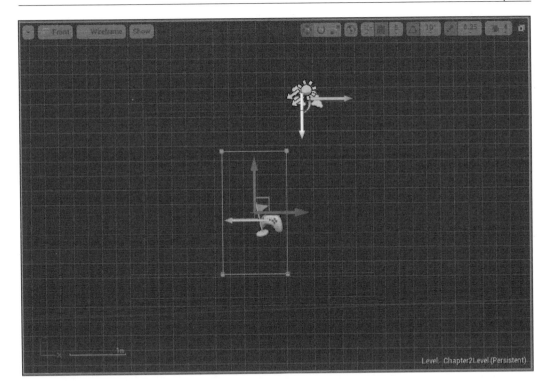

Adding materials to the walls

To make the ground look more realistic, we will apply a material to it. Go to **Content Browser | Content | StarterContent | Materials**. Type Wall into the **Filters** box. Select **M_Basic_Wall** and drag it onto the surface of the wall with the door. Then, we will use a different material. Type Brick into the **Filters** box. Select **M_Brick_Clay_New** to apply to the inner surface of the two other walls.

Here, you can take a look at how the level looks in the **Unlit** mode after applying the materials mentioned previously:

Build the light before running the level again to see how the level looks now.

Sealing a room

For now, let's duplicate the wall with the door to seal the room. Click on the wall, hold down *Alt + Shift*, and drag it across to the other side of the room. The following screenshot shows how it looks when the room is sealed:

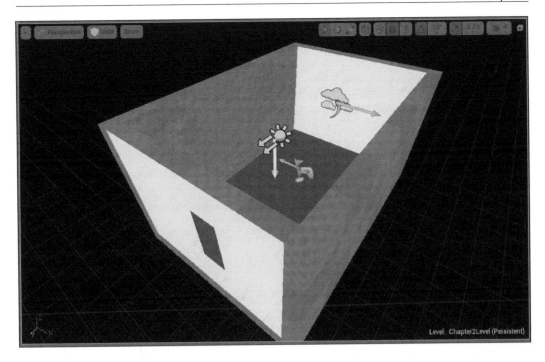

Adding props or a static mesh to the room

Let's now add some objects to the empty room. Go to **Content Browser** | **Content** | **StarterContent** | **Props**. Find **SM_Lamp_Ceiling** and drag it into the room.

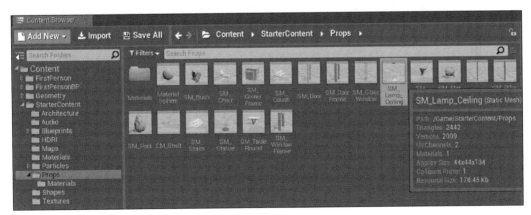

As we want to use a ceiling lamp prop as a floor lamp, you will need to rotate the lamp by rotating it about the *x* axis by 180 degrees. Set X = 180 degrees using the **Relative** mode. The following screenshot shows the rotated lamp positioned at one end of the room. Note that I have built the light and changed the view mode to the **Lit** mode. Feel free to position the lamp anywhere to see how it looks.

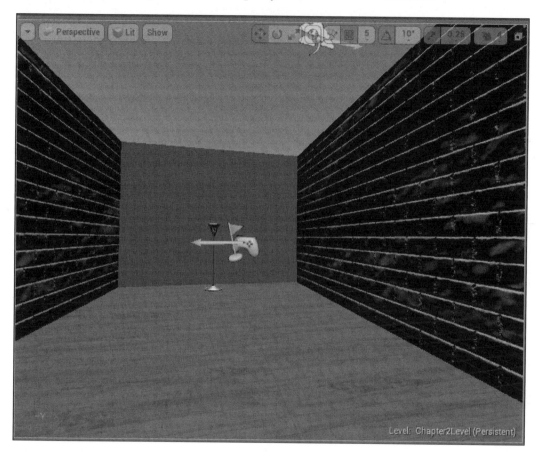

Adding Lightmass Importance Volume

Since our room only takes up a small portion of the map, we can concentrate light on a small region by adding an item known as **Lightmass Importance Volume** to the map. The bounded box of the **Lightmass Importance Volume** tells the engine where light is needed in the map so it should encompass the entire area of the map that has objects. Drag and drop **Lightmass Importance Volume** into the map. Here, you can see where to find the **Lightmass Importance Volume**:

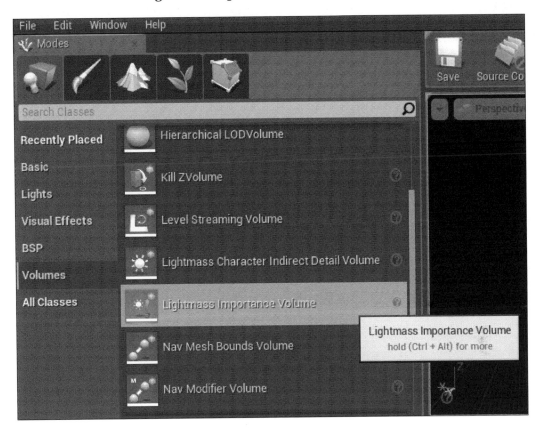

By default, the wireframe box that's been dropped (which is the **Lightmass Importance Volume**) is a cube. You will need to scale it to fit your room. With the **Lightmass Importance Volume** selected, press *R* to display the **Scale** tool. Use the *x*, *y*, and *z* axes to adjust the size of the box till it fits the level. The following screenshot shows the scaling of the box using the **Scale** tool:

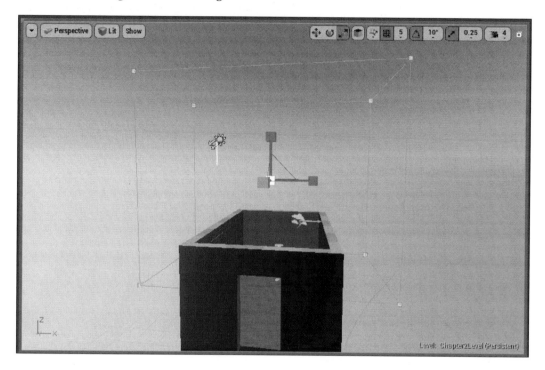

After scaling and translating the box to fit the level, the **Lightmass Importance Volume** should look something like what is shown in the following screenshot, where the wireframe box is large enough to fit the room inside it. The size of the wireframe for the **Lightmass Importance Volume** can be larger than the map.

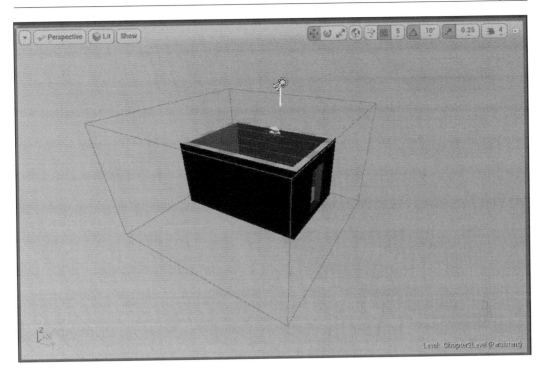

Applying finishing touches to a room

Our room is almost complete. You would have noticed that the door now is just a hole in the wall. To make it look like a door, we need to add a door frame and a door as follows:

1. Go to **Content Browser** | **Content** | **StarterContent** | **Props**.
2. Click and drop **SM_DoorFrame** into the viewport.
3. Adjust it to fit in the wall.

When done, it should look like what is shown in the following screenshot.

I've used different views, such as top, side, and front, to adjust the frame nicely to fit the door. You can adjust **Snap Sizes** for some fine-tuning.

Useful tip – using the drag snap grid

To help you move objects into position more accurately, you can make use of the snap grid button at the top of the viewport as shown in the following screenshot. Turning the drag snap grid on allows you to translate objects according to the grid size you select. Click on the mesh-like symbol to toggle snap grid on/off. The numbers displayed on the right are the minimum grid sizes by which an object will move when translated.

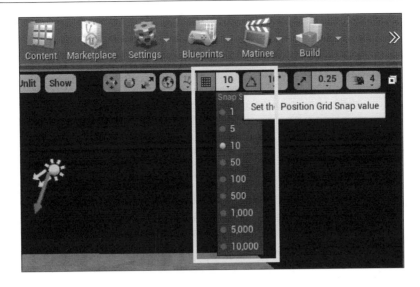

I have also noticed that a portion of the floor is not textured yet. Use the same wood texture as you did previously to make sure that the ground is fully textured using **M_Wood_Floor_Walnut_Polished**.

Then, click and drag **SM_Door** into the viewport. Rotate the door and fit it into the door frame in the same manner as shown previously. Here, you can see how the door is in place:

Summary

We have learned how to navigate the viewport and set up/save a new map in a new project. We also created our first room with a door using the BSP Box brush, added materials to texture walls and floors, and learned to place static objects to enhance the look of the room. Although it is still kind of empty right now, we will continue to work on it in the next few chapters and expand on this map. In the next chapter, we will spice up the level by adding some objects that we can interact with.

3
Game Objects – More and Move

We created our first room in the Unreal Editor in *Chapter 2*, *Creating Your First Level*. In this chapter, we will cover some information about the structure of objects we have used to prototype the level in *Chapter 2*, *Creating Your First Level*. This is to ensure that you have a solid foundation in some important core concepts before moving forward. Then, we will progressively introduce various concepts to make the objects move upon a player's interaction.

In this chapter, we will cover the following topics:

- BSP Brush
- Static Mesh
- Texture and Materials
- Collision
- Volumes
- Blueprint

BSP Brush

We used the BSP Box Brush in *Chapter 2*, *Creating Your First Level*, extensively to create the ground and the walls.

BSP Brushes are the primary building blocks for level creation in the game development. They are used for quick prototyping levels like how we have used them in *Chapter 2*, *Creating Your First Level*.

In Unreal, BSP Brushes come in the form of primitives (box, sphere, and so on) and also predefined/custom shapes.

Background

BSP stands for **binary space partitioning**. The structure of a BSP tree allows spatial information to be accessed quickly for rendering, especially in 3D scenes made up of polygons. A scene is recursively divided into two, until each node of the BSP tree contains only polygons that can render in arbitrary order. A scene is rendered by traversing down the BSP tree from a given node (viewpoint).

Since a scene is divided using the BSP principle, placing objects in the level could be viewed as cutting into the BSP partitions in the scene. Geometry Brushes use **Constructive Solid Geometry (CSG)** technique to create polygon surfaces. CSG combines simple primitives/custom shapes using Boolean operators such as union, subtraction, and intersection to create complex shapes in the level.

So, the CSG technique is used to create surfaces of the object in the level, and rendering the level is based on processing these surfaces using the BSP tree. This relationship has resulted in Geometry Brushes being known also as BSP Brushes, but more accurately, CSG surfaces.

Brush type

BSP Brushes can either be additive or subtractive in nature. Additive brushes are like volumes that fill up the space. Additive brushes were used for the ground and the walls in our map in *Chapter 2, Creating Your First Level*.

Subtractive brushes can be used to form hollow spaces. These were used to create a hole in the wall in which to place a door and its frame in *Chapter 2, Creating Your First Level*.

Brush solidity

For additive brushes, there are various states it can be in: solid, semi-solid, or non-solid.

Since subtractive brushes create empty spaces, players are allowed to move freely within them. Subtractive brushes can only be solid brushes.

Refer to the following table for comparison of their properties:

Brush solidity	Brush type	Degree of blocking	BSP cutting
Solid	Additive and subtractive	Blocks both players and projectiles	Creates BSP cuts to the surrounding world geometry
Semi-solid	Additive only	Blocks both players and projectiles	Does not cause BSP cuts to the surrounding world geometry
Non-solid	Additive only	Does not block players or projectiles	Does not cause BSP cuts to the surrounding world geometry

Static Mesh

Static Mesh is a geometry made up of polygons. Looking more microscopically at what a mesh is made of, it is made up of lines connecting vertices.

Static Mesh has vertices that cannot be animated. This means is that you cannot animate a part of the mesh and make that part move relative to itself. But the entire mesh can be translated, rotated, and scaled. The lamp and the door that we have added in *Chapter 2, Creating Your First Level*, are examples of Static Meshes.

A higher-resolution mesh has more polygons as compared to a lower-resolution mesh. This also implies that a higher resolution mesh has a larger number of vertices. A higher resolution mesh takes more time to render but is able to provide more details in the object.

Static Meshes are usually first created in external software programs, such as Maya or 3ds Max, and then imported into Unreal for placement in game maps.

The door, its frame, and the lamp that we added in *Chapter 2, Creating Your First Level*, are Static Meshes. Notice that these objects are not simple geometry looking objects.

BSP Brush versus Static Mesh

In game development, many objects in the game are Static Meshes. Why is that so? Static Mesh is considered more efficient, especially for a complex object with many vertices, as they can be cached to a video memory and are drawn by the computer's graphics card. So, Static Meshes are preferred when creating objects as they have better render performance, even for complex objects. However, this does not mean that BSP Brushes do not have a role in creating games.

When BSP Brush is simple, it can still be used without causing too much serious impact to the performance. BSP Brush can be easily created in the Unreal Editor, hence it is very useful for quick prototyping by the game/level designers. Simple BSP Brushes can be created and used as temporary placeholder objects while the actual Static Mesh is being modeled by the artists. The creation of a Static Mesh takes time, even more so for a highly detailed Static Mesh. We will cover a little information about the Static Mesh creation pipeline later in this chapter, so we have an idea of the amount of work that needs to be done to get a Static Mesh into the game. So, BSP Brush is great for an early game play testing without having to wait for all Static Meshes to be created.

Making Static Mesh movable

Let us open our saved map that we have created in *Chapter 2, Creating Your First Level*, and let us first save the level as a new `Chapter3Level`.

1. Go to **Content Browser** | **Content** | **StarterContent** | **Props,** and search for **SM_Chair,** which is a standard Static Mesh prop. Click and drag it into our map.

2. The chair we have in the level now is unmovable. You can quickly build and run the level to check it out. To make it movable, we need to change a couple of settings under the chair's details.

3. First, ensure **SM_Chair** is selected, go to the **Details** tab. Go to **Transform** | **Mobility**, change it from **Static** to **Movable**. Take a look at the following screenshot, which describes how to make the chair movable:

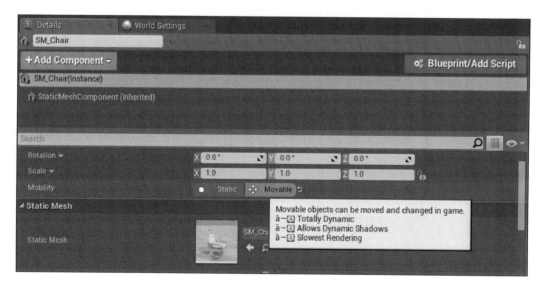

4. Next, we want the chair to be able to respond to us. Scroll a little down the **Details** tab to change the **Physics** setting for the chair. Go to **Details | Physics**. Make sure the checkbox for **Simulate Physics** is checked. When this checkbox is checked, the auto-link setting sets the **Collision** to be a **PhysicsActor**. The following screenshot shows the **Physics** settings of the chair:

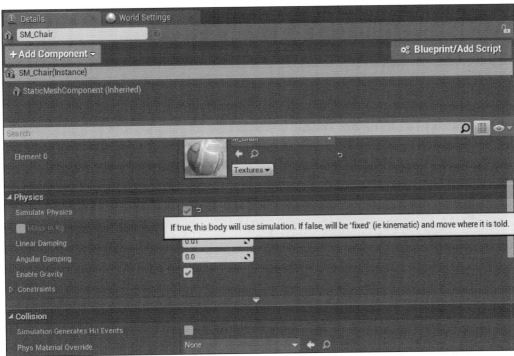

Let us now build and play the level. When you walk into the chair, you will be able to push it around. Just to note, the chair is still known as Static Mesh, but it is now movable.

Materials

In *Chapter 2*, *Creating Your First Level*, we selected a walnut polished material and applied it to the ground. This changed the simple dull ground into a brown polished wood floor. Using materials, we are able to change the look and feel of the objects.

The reason for a short introduction of materials here is because it is a concept that we need to have learned about before we can construct a Static Mesh. We already know that we need Static Meshes in the game and we cannot only rely on the limited selection that we have in the default map package. We will need to know how to create our own Static Meshes, and we rely heavily on Materials to give the Static Meshes their look and feel.

So, when do we apply Materials while creating our custom Static Mesh? Materials are applied to the Static Mesh during its creation process outside the editor, which we will cover in a later section of this chapter. For now, let us first learn how Materials are constructed in the editor.

Creating a Material in Unreal

To fully understand the concept of a Material, we need to break it down into its fundamental components. How a surface looks is determined by many factors, including color, presence of print/pattern/designs, reflectivity, transparency, and many more. These factors combine together to give the surface its unique look.

In Unreal Engine, we are able to create our very own material by using the Material Editor. Based on the explanation given earlier, a Material is determined by many factors and all these factors combine together to give the Material its own look and feel.

Unreal Engine offers a base Material node that has a list of customizable factors, which we can use to design our Material. By using different values to different factors, we can come up with our very own Material. Let us take a look at what is behind the scene in a material that we have used in *Chapter 2, Creating Your First Level*.

Go to **Content Browser** | **Content** | **Starter Content** | **Materials** and double-click on **M_Brick_Clay_New**. This opens up the Material Editor. The following screenshot shows the zoomed-in version of the base Material node for the brick clay material. You might notice that **Base Color**, **Roughness**, **Normal**, and **Ambient Occlusion** have inputs to the base **M_Brick_Clay_New** material node. These inputs make the brick wall look like a brick wall.

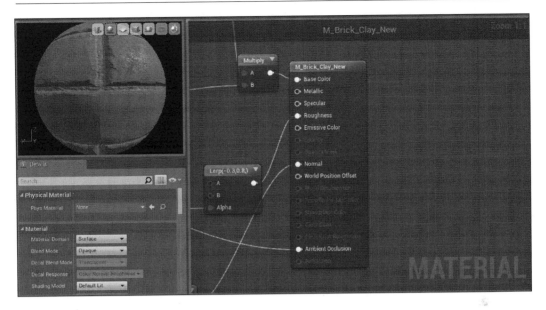

The inputs to these nodes can take on values from various sources. Take **Base Color** for example, we can define the color using RGB values or we can take the color from the texture input. Textures are images in formats, such as `.bmp`, `.jpg`, `.png`, and so on, which we can create using tools, such as Photoshop or ZBrush.

We will talk more about the construction of the materials a little later in this book. For now, let us just keep in mind that materials are applied to the surfaces and textures are what we can use in combination, to give the materials its overall visual look.

Materials versus Textures

Notice that I have used both Materials and Textures in the previous section. It has often caused quite a bit of confusion for a newbie in the game development. Material is what we apply to surfaces and they are made up of a combination of different textures. Materials take on the properties from the textures depending on what was specified, including color, transparency, and so on.

As explained earlier, Textures are simple images in formats such as `.tga`, `.bmp`, `.jpg`, `.png`, and so on.

Texture/UV mapping

Now, we understand that a custom material is made up of a combination of textures and material is applied onto surfaces to give the polygon meshes its identity and realism. The next question is how do we apply these numerous textures that come with the material onto the surfaces? Do we simply slap them onto the 3D object? There must be a predictable manner in which we paint these textures onto the surfaces. The method used is called **Texture Mapping**, which was pioneered by Edwin Catmull in 1974.

Texture mapping assigns pixels from a texture image to a point on the surface of the polygon. The texture image is called a **UV texture map**. The reason we are using UV as an alternative to the XY coordinates is because we are already using XY to describe the geometric space of the object. So the UV coordinates are the texture's XY coordinates, and it is solely used to determine how to paint a 3D surface.

How to create and use a Texture Map

We will first need to unwrap a mesh at its seams and lay it out flat in 2D. This 2D surface is then painted upon to create the texture. This painted texture (also known as **Texture Map**) will then be wrapped back around the mesh by assigning the UV coordinates of the texture on each face of the mesh. To help you better visualize, take a look at the following illustration:

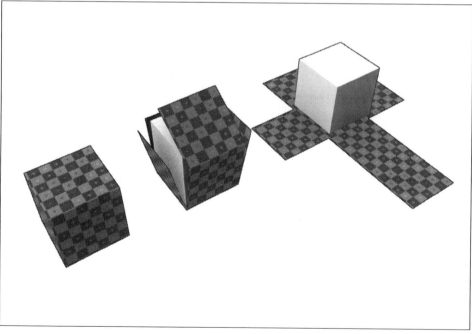

Source: Wikipedia (https://en.wikipedia.org/wiki/UV_mapping)

As a result of this, shared vertices can have more than one set of UV coordinates assigned.

Multitexturing

To create a better appearance in surfaces, we can use multiple textures to create the eventual end result desired. This layering technique allows for many different textures to be created using different combinations of textures. More importantly, it gives the artists better control of details and/or lighting on a surface.

A special form of texture maps – Normal Maps

Normal Maps are a type of texture maps. They give the surfaces little bumps and dents. Normal Maps add the details to the surfaces without increasing the number of polygons. One very effective use of Normal Mapping is to generate Normal Maps from a high polygon 3D model and use it to texture the lower polygon model, which is also known as **baking**. We will discuss why we need the same 3D model with different number of polygons in the next section.

Normal maps are commonly stored as regular RGB images where the RGB components correspond to the X, Y, and Z coordinates, respectively, of the surface normal. The following image shows an example of a normal map taken from `http://www.bricksntiles.com/textures/`:

Level of detail

We create objects with varying **level of details** (**LODs**) to increase the efficiency of rendering. For objects that are closer to the player, high LODs objects are rendered. Objects with higher LODs have a higher number of polygons. For objects that are far away from the player, a simpler version of the object is rendered instead.

Artists can create different LOD versions of the 3D object using automated LOD algorithms, deployed through software or manually reducing the number of vertices, normals, edges in the 3D Models, to create a lower polygon count model. When creating models of different LODs, note that we always start by creating the most detailed model with the most number of polygons first and then reduce the number accordingly to create the other LOD versions. It is much harder to work the models the other way around. Do remember to keep the UV coherent when working with objects with different LODs. Currently, different LODs need to be light mapped separately.

The following image is taken from `http://renderman.pixar.com/view/level-of-detail` and very clearly shows the polygon count based on the distance away from the camera:

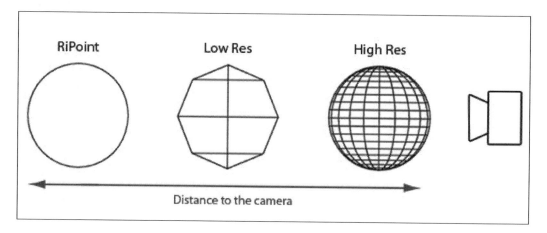

Collisions

Objects in Unreal Engine have collision properties that can be modified to design the behavior of the object when it collides with another object.

In real life, collisions occur when two objects move and meet each other at a point of contact. Their individual object properties will determine what kind of collision we get, how they respond to the collision, and their path after the collision. This is what we try to achieve in the game world as well.

The following screenshot shows the collision properties available to an object in
Unreal Engine 4:

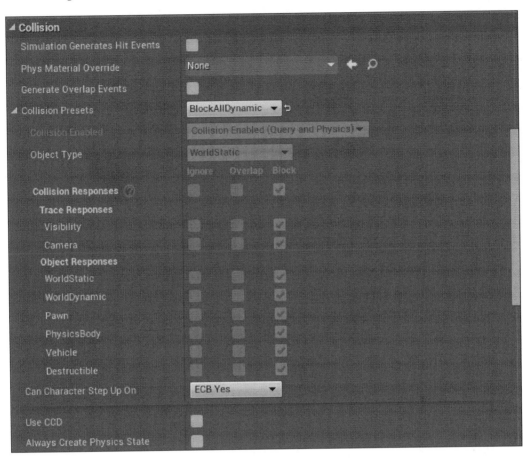

If you are still confused about the concept of collision, imagine Static Mesh to
give an object its shape (how large it is, how wide it is, and so on), while the collision
of the object is able to determine the behavior of this object when placed on the
table—whether the object is able to fall through the table in the level or lay stationery
on the table.

Collision configuration properties

Let us go through some of the possible configurations in Unreal's **Collision**
properties that we should get acquainted with.

Simulation Generates Hit Events

When an object has the **Simulation Generates Hit Events** flag checked, an alert is raised when the object has a collision. This alert notification can be used to trigger the onset of other game actions based on this collision.

Generate Overlap Events

The **Generate Overlap Events** flag is similar to the **Simulation Generates Hit Events** flag, but when this flag is checked, in order to generate an event, all the object needs is to have another object to overlap with it.

Collision Presets

The **Collision Presets** property contains a few frequently used settings that have been preconfigured for you. If you wish to create your own custom collision properties, set this to **Custom**.

Collision Enabled

The **Collision Enabled** property allows three different settings: **No Collision, No Physics Collision**, and **Collision Enabled**. **No Physics Collision** is selected when this object is used only for non-physical types of collision such as raycasts, sweeps, and overlaps. **Collision Enabled** is selected when physics collision is needed. No Collision is selected when absolutely no collision is wanted.

Object Type

Objects can be categorized into several groups: **WorldStatic, WorldDynamic, Pawn, PhysicsBody, Vehicle, Destructible**, and **Projectile**. The type selected determines the interactions it takes on as it moves.

Collision Responses

The **Collision Responses** option sets the property values for all **Trace** and **Object Responses** that come with it. When **Block** is selected for **Collision Responses**, all the properties under **Trace** and **Object Responses** are also set to **Block**.

Trace Responses

The **Trace Responses** option affects how the object interacts with traces. **Visibility** and **Camera** are the two types of traces that you can choose to block, overlap, or ignore.

Object Responses

The **Object Responses** option affects how this object interacts with other object types. Remember the **Object Type** selection earlier? The **Object Type** property determines the type of object, and under this category, you can configure the collision response this object has with the different types of objects.

Collision hulls

For a collision to occur in Unreal Engine, hulls are used. To view an example of the collision hull for a Static Mesh, take a look at the light blue lines surrounding the cube in the following screenshot; it's a box collision hull:

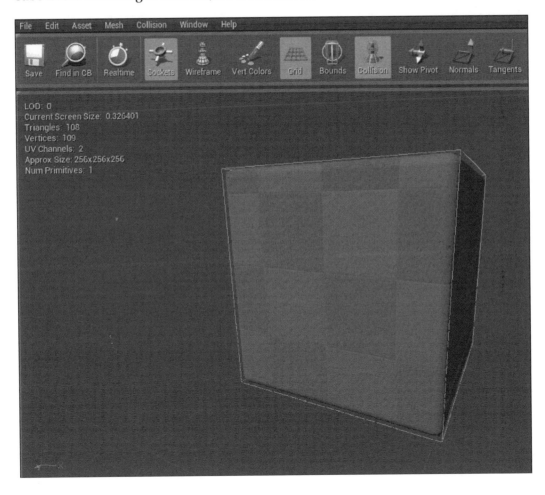

Hulls can be generated in Static Mesh Editor for static meshes. The following screenshot shows the menu options available for creating an auto-generated collision hull in Static Mesh Editor:

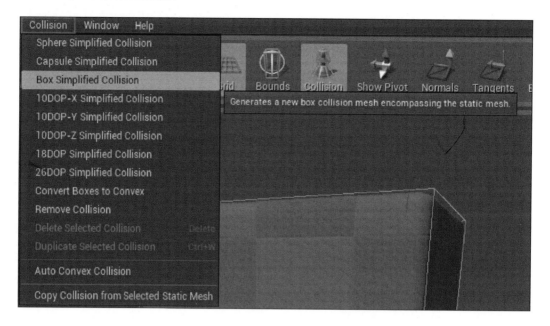

Simple geometry objects can be combined and overlapped to form a simple hull. A simple hull/bounding box reduces the amount of calculation it needs during a collision. So for complex objects, a generalized bounding box can be used to encompass the object. When creating static mesh that has a complex shape, not a simple geometry type of object, you will need to refer to the *Static Mesh creation pipeline* section later on in the chapter to learn how to create a suitable collision bounding box for it.

Interactions

When designing collisions, you will also need to decide what kind of interactions the object has and what it will interact with.

To block means they will collide, and to overlap can mean that no collision will occur. When a block or an overlap happens, it is possible to flag the event so that other actions resulting from this interaction can be taken. This is to allow customized events, which you can have in game.

Note that for a block to actually occur, both objects must be set to **Block** and they must be set so that they block the right type of objects too. If one is set to block and the other to overlap, the overlap will occur but not the block. Block and overlap can happen when objects are moving at a high speed, but events can only be triggered on either overlap or block, not both. You can also set the blocking to ignore a particular type of object, for example, **Pawn**, which is the player.

Static Mesh creation pipeline

Static Mesh creation pipeline is done outside of the editor using 3D modeling tools such as Autodesk's Maya and 3D's Max. Unreal Engine 4 is compatible to import the FBX 2013 version of the files.

This creation pipeline is used mainly by the artists to create game objects for the project.

The actual steps and naming convention when importing Static Mesh into the editor are well documented on the Unreal 4 documentation website. You may refer to `https://docs.unrealengine.com/latest/INT/Engine/Content/FBX/StaticMeshes/index.html` for more details.

Introducing volumes

Volumes are invisible areas that are created to help the game developers perform a certain function. They are used in conjunction with the objects in the level to perform a specific purpose. Volumes are commonly used to set boundaries that are intended to prevent players from gaining access to trigger events in the game, or use the Lightmass Importance Volume to change how light is calculated within an area in the map as in *Chapter 2*, *Creating Your First Level*.

Here's a list of the different types of volumes that can be customized and used in Unreal Engine 4. But feel free to quickly browse through each of the volumes here for now, and revisit them later when we start learning how to use them later in the book. For this chapter, you may focus your attention first on the Trigger Volume, as we will be using that in the later examples of this chapter.

Blocking Volume

The Blocking Volume can be used to prevent players/characters/game objects from entering a certain area of the map. It is quite similar to collision hull which we have described earlier and can be used in place of Static Mesh collision hull, as they are simpler in shapes (block shapes), hence easier to calculate the response of the collision. These volumes also have the ability to detect which objects overlap with themselves quickly.

An example of the usage of the Blocking Volume is to prevent the player from walking across a row of low bushes. In this case, since the bushes are rather irregularly shaped but are roughly forming a straight line, like a hedge, an invisible Blocking Volume would be a very good way of preventing the player from crossing the bushes.

The following screenshot shows the properties for the Blocking Volume. We can change the shape and size of the volume under **Brush Settings**. Collision events and triggers other events using Blueprint. This is pretty much the basic configuration we will get for all other volumes too.

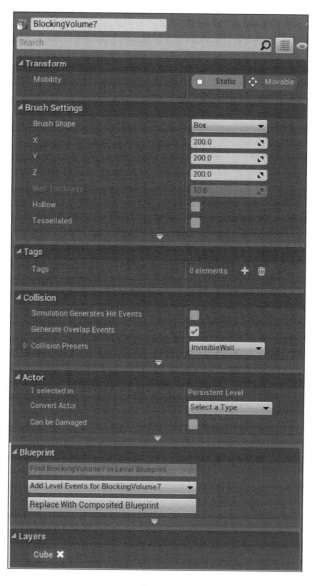

Camera Blocking Volume

The Camera Blocking Volume works in the same way as the Blocking Volume but it is used specifically to block cameras. It is useful when you want to limit the player from exploring with the camera beyond a certain range.

Trigger Volume

The Trigger Volume is probably one of the most used volumes. This is also the volume which we would be using to create events for the game level that we have been working on. As the name implies, upon entering this volume, we can trigger events, and via Blueprint, we can create a variety of events for our game, such as moving an elevator or spawning NPCs.

Nav Mesh Bounds Volume

The Nav Mesh Bounds Volume is used to indicate the space in which NPCs are able to freely navigate around. NPCs could be enemies in the game who need some sort of path finding method to get around the level on their own. This Nav Mesh Bounds Volume will set up the area in the game that they are able to walk through. This is important as there could be obstacles such as bridges that they will need to use to in order get across to the other side (instead of walking straight into the river and possibly drowning).

Physics Volume

The Physics Volume is used to create areas in which the physics properties of the player/objects in the level change. An example of this would be altering the gravity within a space ship only when it reaches the orbit. When the gravity is changed in these areas, the player starts to move slower and float in the space ship. We can then turn this volume off when the ship comes back to earth. The following screenshot shows the additional settings we get from the Physics Volume:

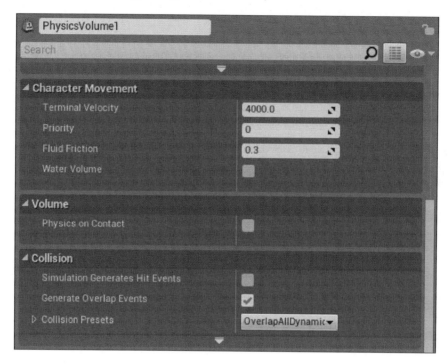

Pain Causing Volume

The Pain Causing Volume is a very specialized volume used to create damage to the players upon entry. It is a "milder" version of the Kill Z Volume. Reduction of health and the amount of damage per second are customizable, according to your game needs. The following screenshot shows the properties you can adjust to control how much pain to inflict on the player:

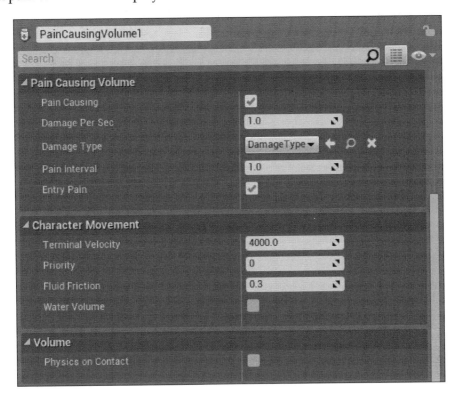

Kill Z Volume

We kill the player when it enters the Kill Z Volume. This is a very drastic volume that kills the player immediately. An example of its usage is to kill the player immediately when the player falls off a high building. The following screenshot shows the properties of Kill Z Volume to determine the point at which the player is killed:

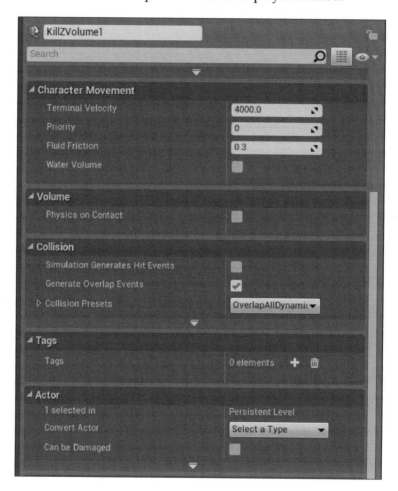

Level Streaming Volume

The Level Streaming Volume is used to display the levels when you are within the volume. It generally fills the entire space where you want the level to be loaded. The reason we need to stream levels is to give players an illusion that we have a large open game level, when in fact the level is broken up into chunks for more efficient rendering. The following screenshot shows the properties that can be configured for the Level Streaming Volume:

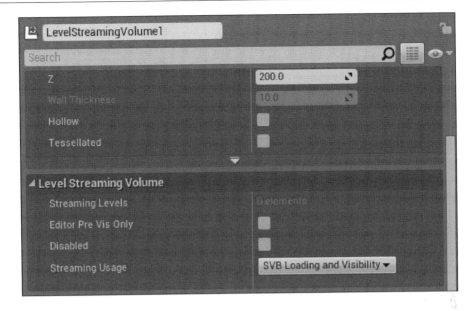

Cull Distance Volume

The Cull Distance Volume allows objects to be culled in the volume. The definition of cull is to select from a group. The Cull Distance Volume is used to select objects in the volume that need to disappear (or not rendered) based on the distance away from the camera. Tiny objects that are far away from the camera cannot be seen visibly. These objects can be culled if the camera is too far away from those objects. Using the Cull Distance Volume, you would be able to decide upon the distance and size of objects, which you want to cull within a fixed space. This can greatly improve performance of your game when used effectively.

This might seem very similar to the idea of occlusion. Occlusion is implemented by selecting object by object, when it is not rendered on screen. These are normally used for larger objects in the scene. Cull Distance Volume can be used over a large area of space and using conditions to specify whether or not the objects are rendered.

The following screenshot shows the configuration settings that are available to the Cull Distance Volume:

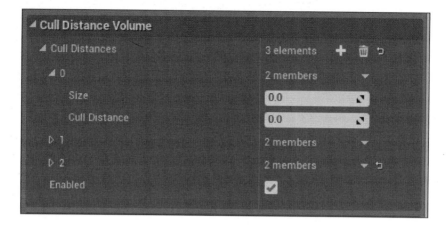

Audio Volume

The Audio Volume is used to mimic real ambient sound changes when one transits from one place to another, especially when transiting to and from very different environments, such as walking into a clock shop from a busy street, or walking in and out of a restaurant with a live band playing in the background.

The volume is placed surrounding the boundaries of one of the areas creating an artificial border dividing the spaces into interior and exterior. With this artificially created boundary and settings that come with this Audio Volume, sound artists are able to configure how sounds are played during this transition.

PostProcess Volume

The PostProcess Volume affects the overall scene using post-processing techniques. Post-processing effects include Bloom effects, Anti-Aliasing, and Depth of Field.

Lightmass Importance Volume

We have used Lightmass Importance Volume in *Chapter 2, Creating Your First Level*, to focus the light on the section of the map that has the objects in. The size of the volume should encompass your entire level.

Introducing Blueprint

The Unreal Editor offers the ability to create custom events for game levels through a visual scripting system. Before Unreal Engine 4, it was known as the **Kismet system**. In Unreal Engine 4, this system was revamped with more features and capabilities. The improved system was launched with the new name of Blueprint.

There are several types of Blueprint: Class Blueprint, Data-Only Blueprint, and Level Blueprint. These are more or less equivalent to what we used to know as Kismet, which is now known as Level Blueprint.

Why do I need Blueprint? The simple answer is that through Blueprint, we are able to control gameplay without having to dive into the actual coding. This makes it convenient for non-programmers to design and modify the gameplay. So, it mainly benefits the game designers/artists who can configure the game through the Blueprint editor.

So, how can we use Blueprint and what can I use Blueprint for? Blueprint is just like coding with an interface. You can select, drag, and drop function nodes into the editor, and link them up logically to evoke the desired response to specified scenarios in your game. For programmers, they will be able to pick it up pretty quickly, since Blueprint is in fact coding but through a visual interface.

For the benefit of everyone who is new to Unreal Engine 4 and maybe programming as well, we will go through a basic example of how Level Blueprint works here and use that as an example to go through some basic programming concepts at the same time.

What will we be using Blueprint for? Blueprint has the capabilities to prototype, implement, or modify virtually any gameplay element. The gameplay elements affect how game objects are spawned, what gets spawned, where they are spawned, and under what conditions they are spawned. The game objects can include lights, camera, player's input, triggers, meshes, and character models. Blueprint can control properties of these game objects dynamically to create countless gameplay scenarios. The examples of usage include altering the color of the lights when you enter a room in the game, triggering the door to shut behind you after entering the room and playing the sound effect of the door closing shut, spawning weapons randomly among three possible locations in the map, and so on.

In this chapter, we will focus on Level Blueprint first, since it is the most commonly used form of Blueprint.

Level Blueprint

Level Blueprint is a type of Blueprint that has influence over what happens in the level. Events that are created in this Blueprint affect what happens in the level, and are made specific to the situation by specifying the particular object it targets.

Feel free to jump to the next section first where we will go through a Blueprint example, so that we are able to understand Level Blueprint a little better.

The following screenshot shows a blank Level Blueprint. The most used window is **Event Graph**, which is in the center. Using different node types in **Event Graph** and linking it up appropriately creates a responsive interaction within the game. The nodes come with variables, values, and other similar properties used in programming to control the game events graphically (without writing a single line of script or code).

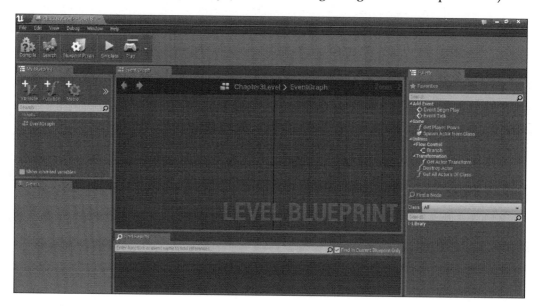

Using the Trigger Volume to turn on/off light

We are now ready to use what we have learned to construct the next room for our game. We will duplicate the first room we have created in order to create our second room.

1. Open the level that we created in *Chapter 2, Creating Your First Level*, (Chapter2_Level) and save it as a new level called Chapter3_Level.

2. Select all the walls, the floor, the door, and the door frame.

3. Hold down *Alt + Shift* and drag to duplicate the room.

4. Place the duplicated room with the duplicated door aligned to the wall of the first room. Refer to the following screenshot to see how the walls are aligned from a **Top** view perspective:

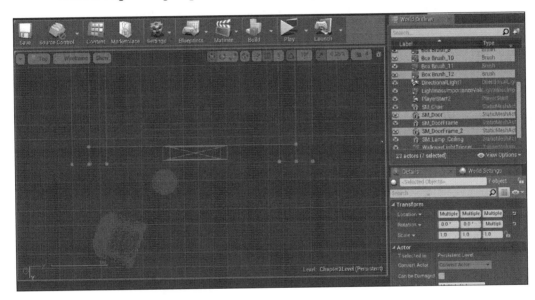

5. Delete the back wall of the first room to link both the rooms.

6. Delete all the doors to allow easy access to the second room.

7. Move the standing lamp and chair to the side. Take a look the following screenshot to understand how the rooms look at this point:

8. Rebuild the lights. The following screenshot shows the room correctly illuminated after building the lights:

9. Now, let us focus on working on the second room. We will create a narrower walkway using the second room that we have just created.

10. Move the sidewalls closer to each other—about 30 cm from the previous sidewall towards the center. Refer to the next two screenshots for the **Top** and **Perspective** views after moving the sidewalls:

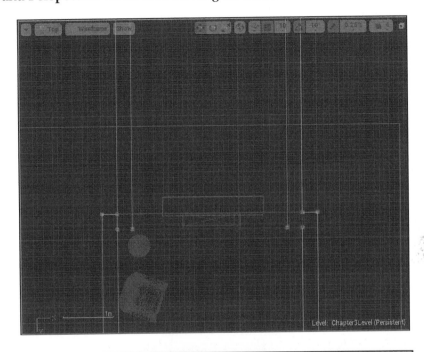

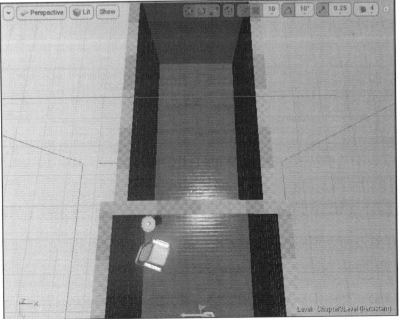

11. Note that LightMass Importance Volume is not encompassing the entire level now. Increase the size of the volume to cover the whole level. Take a look at the following screenshot to see how to extend the size of the volume correctly:

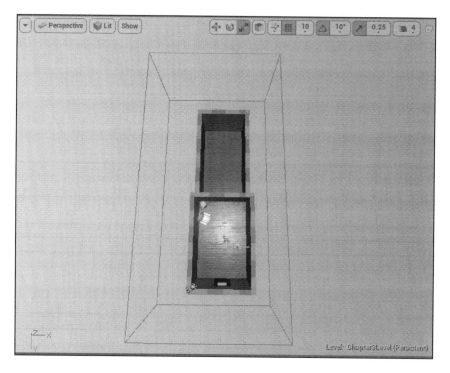

12. Go to **Content Browser | Props**. Click and drop **SM_Lamp_Wall** into the level. Rotate the lamp if necessary so that it lies nicely on the side wall.

13. Go to **Modes | Lights**. Click and drop a Point Light into the second room. Place it just above the light source on the wall light, which we added in the previous step. Take a look at the following screenshot to see the placement of the lamp and Point Light that we have just added:

14. Adjust the Point Light settings: Intensity = 1700.0. This is approximately the light intensity coming off a light bulb. The following screenshot shows the settings for the Point Light:

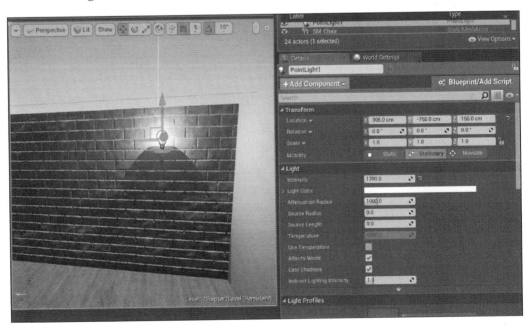

15. Next, go to **Light Color** and adjust the color of the light to **#FF9084FF**, to adjust the mood of the level.

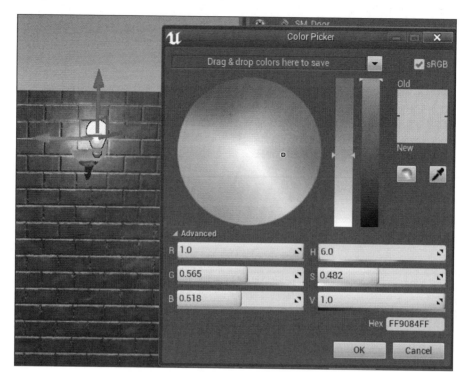

16. Now, let us rename the Point Light to `WalkwayLight` and the **Wall Lamp prop** to `WallLamp`.

17. Select the Point Light and right-click to display the contextual menu. Go to **Attach To** and select **WallLamp**. This attaches the light to the prop so that when we move the prop, the light moves together. The following screenshot shows that **WalkwayLight** is linked to **WallLamp**:

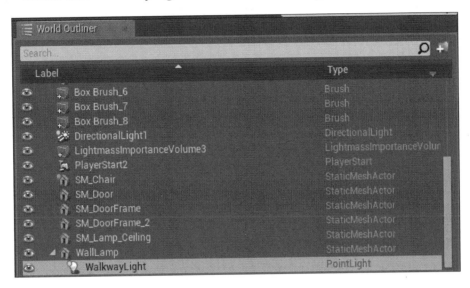

18. Now, let us create a Trigger Volume. Go to **Modes | Volumes**. Click and drag the Trigger Volume into the level.

19. Resize the volume to cover the entrance of the door dividing the two rooms. Refer to the next two screenshots on how to position the volume (**Perspective** view and **Top** view). Make sure that the volume covers the entire space of the door.

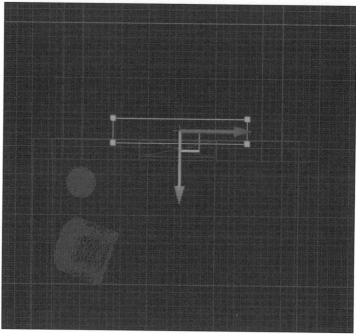

20. Rename **Trigger Volume** to `WalkwayLightTrigger`.

21. In order to use the Trigger Volume to turn the light on and off, we need to figure out which property from the Point Light controls this feature. Click on the Point Light (**WalkwayLight**) to display the properties of the light. Scroll down to **Rendering** and uncheck the property box for **Visible**. Notice that the light is now turned off. We want to keep the light turned off until we trigger it.

22. So, the next step is to link the sequence of events up. This is done via **Level Blueprint**. We will need to trigger this change in property using the Trigger Volume, which we have created and turn the light back on.

23. With the Point Light still selected, go to the top ribbon and select **Blueprints | Open Level Blueprint**. This opens up the **Level Blueprint** window. Make sure that the Point Light (**WalkwayLight**) is still selected as shown in the following screenshot:

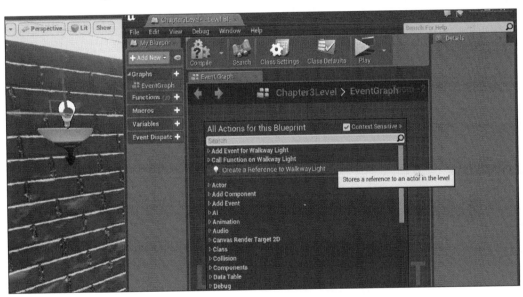

24. Right-click in the **Event Graph** of the **Level Blueprint** window to display what actions can be added to the **Level Blueprint**.

25. Due to Level Blueprint's ability to guide what actions are possible, we can simply select **Add Reference to WalkwayLight**. This creates the **WalkwayLight** actor in **Level Blueprint**. The following screenshot shows the **WalkwayLight** actor correctly added in **Blueprint**:

26. You can keep the **Level Blueprint** window open, and go to the Trigger Volume we have created the in the level.

27. Select the Trigger Volume (**WalkwayLightTrigger**), right-click and select **Add Event** and then **OnActorBeginOverlap**. The following screenshot shows how to add **OnActorBeginOverlap** in **Level Blueprint**:

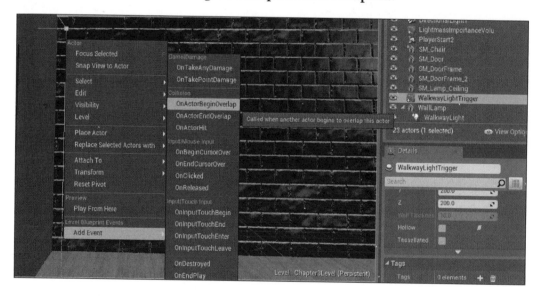

28. To control a variable in the Point Light, we will click and drag on the tiny blue circle on the **WalkwayLight** node added. This creates a blue line originating from the tiny blue circle. This also opens up a menu, where we can see what action can be done to the Point Light. Enter `visi` into the search bar to display the options. Click on **Set Visibility**. The following screenshot shows how to add the **Set Visibility** function to the Point Light (**WalkwayLight**):

29. Check the **New Visiblity** checkbox in the **Set Visiblity** function. The following screenshot shows the configuration we want:

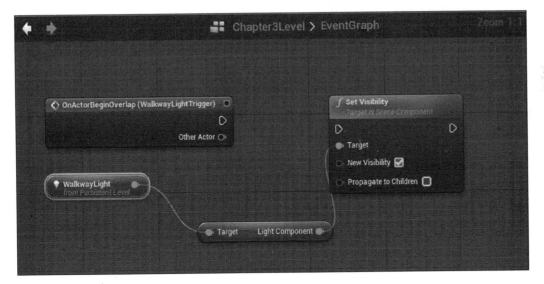

30. Now, we are ready to link the **OnActorBeginOverlap** event to the **Set Visibility** function. Click and drag the white triangular box from **OnActorBeginOverlap** and drop it on the white triangular box at the **Set Visibility** function. The following screenshot shows the event correctly linked up:

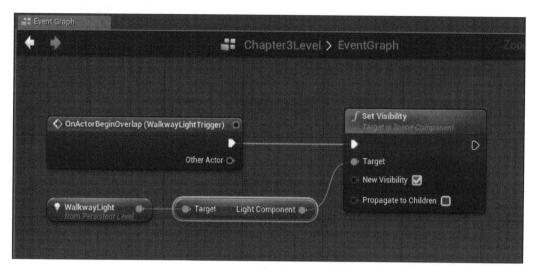

31. Now, build the level and play. Walk through the door from the first room to the second room. The light should be triggered on.

But what happens when you walk back into the first room? The light remained turned on and nothing happens when you walk back into the second room. In the next example, we will go through how you can toggle the light on and off as you walk in and out the room. It is an alternative way to implement the control of the light and I shall leave it as optional for you to try it out.

Using Trigger Volume to toggle light on/ off (optional)

The following steps can be used to trigger volume to toggle lights on or off:

1. We need to replace the **Set Visibility** node in **Event Graph**. Click and drag the blue dot from Point Light (**WalkwayLight**) and drop it onto any blank space. This opens up the contextual menu. The following screenshot shows the contextual menu to place a new node from **WalkwayLight**:

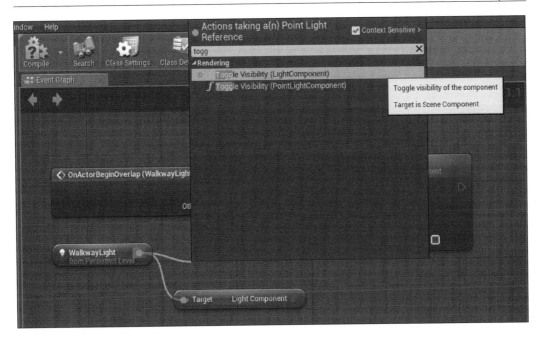

2. Select **Toggle Visibility**. This creates an additional new node in **Event Graph**; we will need to rewire the links as per the following screenshot in order to link **OnActorBeginOverlap** to **Toggle Visibility**:

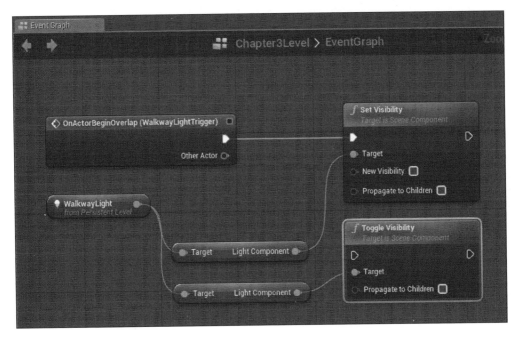

3. The last step is to delete the **Set Visiblity** node and we are ready to toggle the light on and off as we move in and out of the room. The following screenshot shows the final **Event Graph** we want. Compile and play the level to see how you can toggle the light on and off.

Summary

We have covered a number of very important concepts about the objects that we use to populate our game world in Unreal Engine 4. We have broken one of the most common types of game object, Static Mesh, into its most fundamental components in order to understand its construction. We have also compared two types of game objects (Static Meshes and BSP), how they are different, and why they have their spot in the game. This will help you decide what kind of objects need to be created and how they will be created for your game level.

The chapter also briefly introduced textures and materials, how they are created, and applied onto the meshes. We will go into more details about Materials in the next chapter. So you might want to read *Chapter 4, Material and Light*, first before creating/applying materials to your newly created game objects. To help you optimize your game, this chapter also covered the mesh creation pipeline and the concept of LOD. For interactions to take place, we also needed to learn how objects interact and collide with one another in Unreal, what object properties are configurable to allow different physics interaction.

This chapter also covered our first introduction to Blueprint, the graphical scripting of Unreal Engine4. Through a simple Blueprint example, we learned how to turn on and off lights for our level using one of the many useful volumes that are in Unreal, Trigger Volume. In the next chapter, we will continue to build on the level we have created with more exciting materials and lights.

4

Material and Light

In this chapter, we will learn in detail about the materials and the lights in Unreal Engine 4. We have grouped both Material and Light together in this chapter because how an object looks is largely determined by both—material and lighting.

Material is what we apply to the surface of an object and it affects how the object looks in the game. Material/Shader programming is a hot ongoing research topic as we always strive to improve the texture performance—seeking higher graphic details/realism/quality with limited CPU/GPU rendering power. Researchers in this area need to find ways to make the models we have in a game look as real as possible, with as little calculations/data size as possible.

Lighting is also a very powerful tool in world creation. There are many uses of light. Lights can create a mood for the level. When effectively used, it can be used to focus attention on objects in the level and guide players through your level. Light also creates shadow. In a game level, shadow needs to be created artificially. Hence, we will also learn how we get shadows rendered appropriately for our game.

Materials

In the previous chapter, we briefly touched on what a material is and what a texture is. A texture is like a simple image file in the format of .png/ .tga. A material is a combination of different elements, including textures to create a surface property that we apply to our objects in the game. We have also briefly covered what UV coordinates are and how we use them to apply a 2D texture to the surface of a 3D object.

So far, we have only learned how to apply materials that are available in the default Unreal Engine. In this chapter, we will dive deeper into how we can actually create our own custom material in Unreal Engine 4. Fundamentally, the material creation for the objects falls into the scope of an artist. For special customized textures, they are sometimes hand painted by 2D artists using tools such as Photoshop or taken from photographs of textures from the exact objects we want, or similar objects. Textures can also be tweaked from existing texture collection to create the customized material that is needed for the 3D models. Due to the vast number of realistic textures needed, textures are sometimes also generated algorithmically by the programmers to allow more control over its final look. This is also an important research area for the advancing materials for computer graphics.

Material manipulation here falls under the scope of a specialized group of programmers known as **graphic programmers**. They are sometimes also researchers that look into ways to better compress texture, improve rendering performance, and create special dynamic material manipulation.

The Material Editor

In Unreal Engine 4, material manipulation can be achieved using the Material Editor. What this editor offers is the ability to create material expressions. Material expressions work together to create an overall surface property for the material. You can think of them as mathematical formulas that add/multiply together to affect the properties of a material. The Material Editor makes it easy to edit/formulate material expressions to create customized material and provides the capability to quickly preview the changes in the game. Through Unreal's Blueprint capabilities and programming, we can also achieve dynamic manipulation of materials as needed by the game.

The rendering system

The rendering system in Unreal Engine 4 uses the DirectX 11 pipeline, which includes deferred shading, global illumination, lit translucency, and post processing. Unreal Engine 4 has also started branching to work with the newest DirectX 12 pipeline for Windows 10, and DirectX 12 capabilities will be available to all.

Physical Based Shading Model

Unreal Engine 4 uses the **Physical Based Shading Model** (PBSP). This is a concept used in many modern day game engines. It uses an approximation of what light does in order to give an object its properties. Using this concept, we give values (0 to 1) to these four properties: **Base Color**, **Roughness**, **Metallic**, and **Specular** to approximate the visual properties.

For example, the bark of a tree trunk is normally brown, rough, and not very reflective. Based on what we know about how the bark should look like, we would probably set the metallic value to low value, roughness to a high value, and the base color to display brown with a low specular value.

This improves the process of creating materials as it is more intuitive as visual properties are governed by how light reacts, instead of the old method where we approximate the visual properties based on how light should behave.

For those who are familiar with the old terms used to describe material properties, you can think of it as having **Diffuse Color** and **Specular Power** replaced by **Base Color**, **Metallic**, and **Roughness**.

The advantage of using PBSP is that we can better approximate material properties with more accuracy.

High Level Shading Language

The Material Editor enables visual scripting of the **High Level Shading Language** (**HLSL**), using a network of nodes and connection. Those who are completely new to the concept of shaders or HLSL should go on to read the next section about shaders, DirectX and HLSL first, so that you have the basic foundation on how the computer renders material information on the screen. HLSL is aproprietary shading language developed by Microsoft. OpenGL has its own version, known as GLSL. HLSL is the programming language used to program the stages in the graphics pipeline. It uses variables that are similar to C programming and has many intrinsic functions that are already written and available for use by simply calling the function.HLSL shaders can be compiled at author-time or at runtime, and set at runtime into the appropriate pipeline stage.

Getting started

To open the Material Editor in Unreal Engine 4, go to **Content Browser | Material** and double-click on any material asset. Alternatively, you can select a material asset, right-click to open the context menu and select **Edit** to view that asset in the Material Editor.

If you want to learn how to create a new material, you can try out the example, which is covered in the upcoming section.

Creating a simple custom material

We will continue to use the levels we have created. Open `Chapter3Level.umap` and rename it `Chapter4Level.umap` to prevent overwriting what we have completed at the end of the previous chapter.

To create a new Material asset in our game package, go to **Content Browser |
Material**. With **Material** selected, right-click to open the contextual menu, navigate
to **New Asset | Material**. This creates the new material in the Material folder
(we want to place assets in logical folders so that we can find game assets easily).
Alternatively, you can go to **Content Browser | New | Material**.

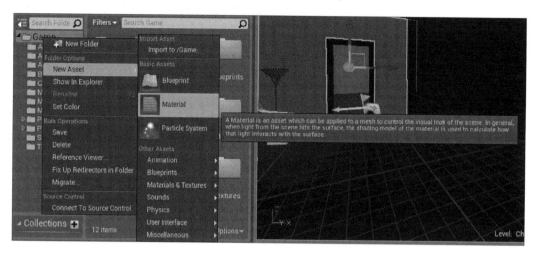

Rename the new material to MyMaterial. The following screenshot shows the new
MyMaterial correctly created:

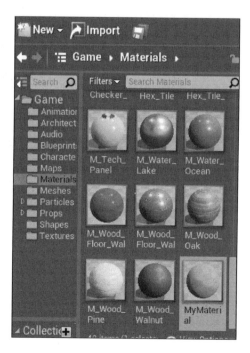

Note that the thumbnail display for the new **MyMaterial** shows a grayed-out checkered material. This is the default material when no material has been applied.

To open the Material Editor to start designing our material, double-click on **MyMaterial**. The following screenshot shows the Material Editor with a blank new material. The spherical preview of the material shows up as black since no properties have been defined yet.

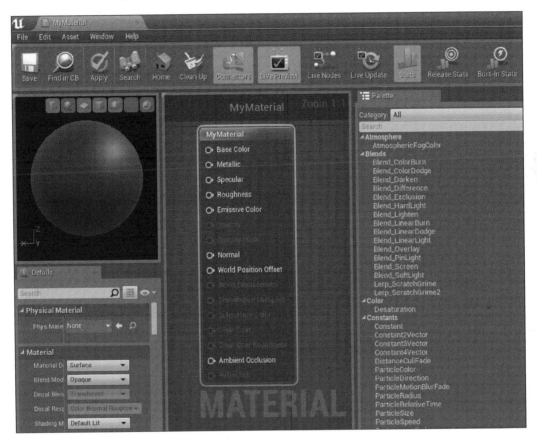

Let's start to define some properties for the **MyMaterial** node to create our very own unique material. **Base Color**, **Metallic**, and **Roughness** are the three values we will learn to configure first.

Base Color is defined by the red, green, and blue values in the form of a vector. To do so, we will drag and drop **Constant3Vector** from **MyPalette** on the right-hand side into the main window where the **MyMaterial** node is in. Alternatively, you can right-click to open the context menu and type `vector` into the search box to filter the list. Click and select **Constant3Vector** to create the node. Double-click on the **Constant3Vector** to display the **Color Picker** window. The following screenshot shows the setting of **Constant3Vector** we want to use to create a material for a red wall. (**R = 0.4, G = 0.0, B = 0.0, H = 0.0, S = 1.0, V = 0.4**):

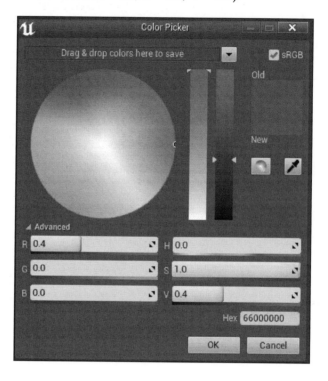

Connect the **Constant3Vector** to the **MyMaterial** node as shown in the following screenshot by clicking and dragging from the small circle from the **Constant3Vector** node to the small circle next to the **Base Color** property in the **MyMaterial** node. This **Constant3Vector** node now provides the base color to the material. Notice how the spherical preview on the left updates to show the new color. If the color is not updated automatically, make sure that the **Live Preview** setting on the top ribbon is selected.

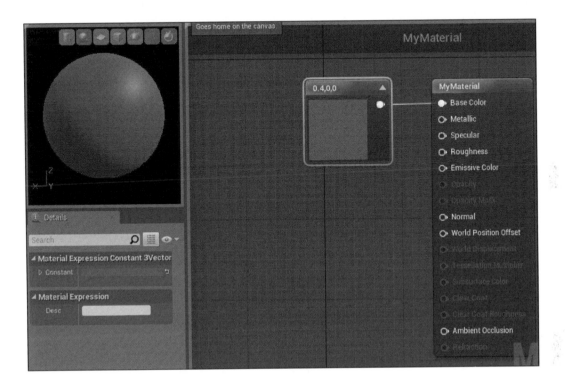

Now, let us set the **Metallic** value for the material. This property takes a numerical value from 0 to 1, where 1 is for a 100% metal. To create an input for a value, click and drag **Constant** from **MyPalette** or right-click in the Material Editor to open the menu; type in Constant into the search box to filter and select **Constant** from the filtered list. To edit the value in the constant, click on the **Constant** node to display the **Details** window and fill in the value. The following screenshot shows how the material would look if **Metallic** is set to 1:

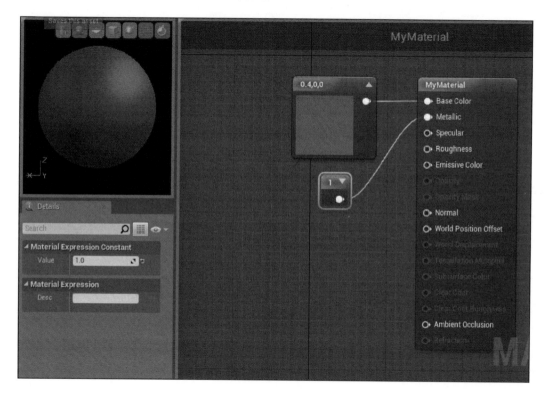

After seeing how the **Metallic** value affects the material, let us see what **Roughness** does. **Roughness** also takes a **Constant** value from 0 to 1, where 0 is completely smooth and makes the surface very reflective. The left-hand screenshot shows how the material looks when **Roughness** is set to 0, whereas the right-hand screenshot shows how the material will look when **Roughness** is set to 1:

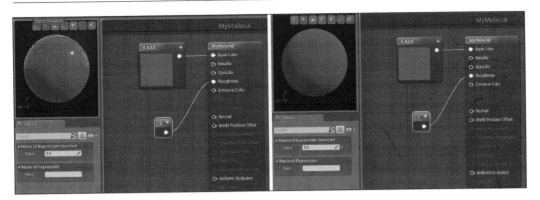

We want to use this new material to texture the walls. So, we have set **Metallic** as **0.3** and **Roughness** as **0.7**. The following screenshot shows the final settings we have for our first custom material:

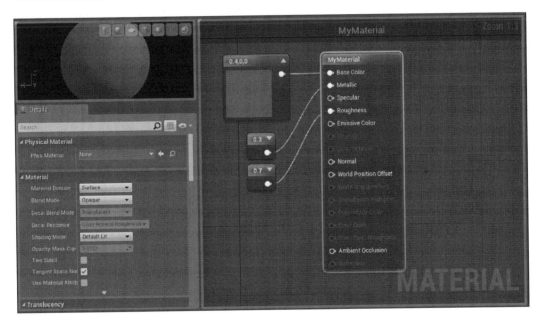

Go to **MyMaterial** in **Content Browser** and duplicate **MyMaterial**. Rename it `MyWall_Grey`. Change the base color to gray using the following values as shown in the picker node for the **Constant3Vector** value for **Base Color**. (R = 0.185, G = 0.185, B = 0.185, H = 0.0, S = 0.0, V = 0.185):

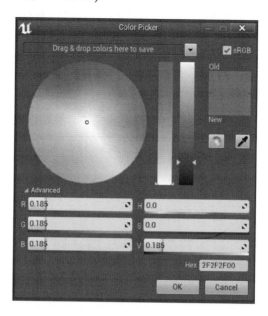

The following screenshot shows the links for the **MyWall_Grey** node. (**Metallic = 0.3, Roughness = 0.7**):

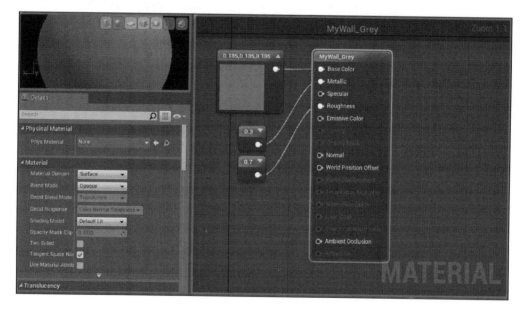

Creating custom material using simple textures

To create a material using textures, we must first select a texture that is suitable. Textures can be created by artists or taken from photos of materials. For learning purposes, you can find suitable free source images from the Web, such as www. textures.com, and use them. Remember to check for conditions of usage and other license-related clauses, if you plan to publish it in a game.

There are two types of textures we need for a custom material using a simple texture. First, the actual texture that we want to use. For now, let us keep this selection simple and straightforward. Select this texture based on the color and it should have the overall properties of what you want the material to look like. Next, we need a normal texture. If you still remember what a normal map is, it controls the bumps on a surface. The normal map gives the grooves in a material. Both of these textures will work together to give you a realistic-looking material that you can use in your game.

In this example, we will create another wood texture that we will use to replace the wood texture from the default package that we have already applied in the room.

Here, we will start first by importing the textures that we need in Unreal Engine. Go to **Content Browser | Textures**. Then click on the **Import** button at the top. This opens up a window to browse to the location of your texture. Navigate to the folder location where your texture is saved, select the texture and click on **Open**. Note that if you are importing textures that are not in the power of two (256 x 256, 1024 x 1024, and so on), you would have a warning message. Textures that are not in the power of two should be avoided due to poor memory usage. If you are importing the example images that I am using, they are already converted to the power of two so you would not get this warning message on screen.

Import both **T_Wood_Light** and **T_Wood_Light_N**. **T_Wood_Light** will be used as the main texture, we want to have, and **T_Wood_Light_N** is the normal map texture, which we will use for this wood.

Next, we follow the same steps to create a new material, as in the previous example. Go to **Content Browser | Material**. With the **Material** folder selected, to open the contextual menu, navigate to **New Asset | Material**. Rename the new material MyWood.

Now, instead of selecting **Constant3Vector** to provide values to the base color, we will use **TextureSample**. Go to **MyPalette** and type in `Texture` to filter the list. Select **TextureSample**, drag and drop it into the Material Editor. Click on the **TextureSample** node to display the **Details** panel, as shown in the following screenshot. On the **Details** panel, go to **Material Expression Texture Base** and click on the small arrow next to it. This opens up a popup with all the suitable assets that you can use. Scroll down to select **T_Wood_Light**.

Now, we have configured **TextureSample** with the wood texture that we have imported into the editor earlier. Connect **TextureSample** by clicking on the white hollow circle connector, dragging it and dropping it on the **Base Color** connector on the **MyWood** node.

Repeat the same steps to create a **TextureSample** node for the **T_Wood_Light_N** normal map texture and connect it to the **Normal** input for **MyWood**.

The following screenshot shows the settings that we want to have for **MyWood**. To have a little glossy feel for our wood texture, set **Roughness** to **0.2** by using a **Constant** node. (Recap: drag and drop a **Constant** node from **MyPalette** and set the value to **0.2**, connect it to the **Roughness** input of **MyWood**.)

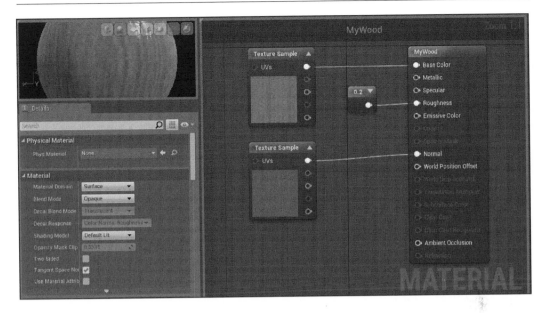

Using custom materials to transform the level

Using the custom materials that we have created in the previous two examples, we will replace the current materials that we have used.

The following screenshot shows the before and after look of the first room. Notice how the new custom materials have transformed the room into a modern looking room.

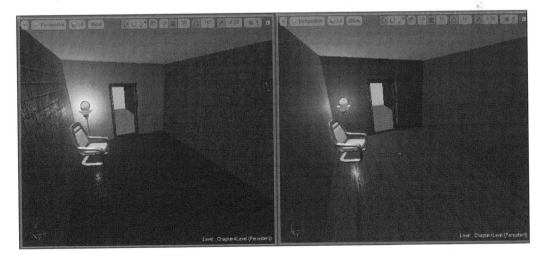

From the preceding screenshot, we also have added a Point Light and placed it onto the lamp prop, making it seem to be emitting light. The following screenshot shows the Point Light setting we have used (**Light Intensity = 1000.0, Attenuation Radius = 1000.0**):

Next, we added a ceiling to cover up the room. The ceiling of the wall uses the same box geometry as the rest of the walls. We have applied the **M_Basic_Wall** material onto it.

Then, we use the red wall material (**MyMaterial**) to replace the material on wall with the door frame. The gray wall material (**MyWall_Grey**) is used to replace the brick material for the walls at the side. The glossy wood material (**MyWood**) is used to replace the wooden floor material.

Rendering pipeline

For an image to appear on the screen, the computer must draw the images on the screen to display it. The sequence of steps to create a 2D representation of a scene by using both 2D and 3D data information is known as the graphics or rendering pipeline. Computer hardware such as **central processing unit** (**CPU**) and **graphics processing unit** (**GPU**) are used to calculate and manipulate the input data needed for drawing the 3D scene.

As games are interactive and rely heavily on real-time rendering, the amount of data necessary for rendering moving scenes is huge. Coordinate position, color, and all display information needs to be calculated for each vertex of the triangle polygon and at the same time, taking into account the effect of overlapping polygons before they can be displayed on screen correctly. Hence, it is very crucial to optimize both the CPU and GPU capabilities to process this data and deliver them timely on the screen. Continuous improvement in this area has been made over the years to allow better quality images to be rendered at higher frame rates for a better visual effect. At this point, games should run at a minimum frame rate of 30fps in order for players to have a reasonable gaming experience.

The rendering pipeline today uses a series of programmable shaders to manipulate information about an image before displaying the image on the screen. We'll cover shaders and Direct3D 11 graphics pipeline in more detail in the upcoming section.

Shaders

Shaders can be thought of as a sequence of programming codes that tells a computer how an image should be drawn. Different shaders govern different properties of an image. For example, Vertex Shaders give properties such as position, color, and UV coordinates for individual vertices. Another important purpose of vertex shaders is to transform vertices with 3D coordinates into the 2D screen space for display. Pixel shaders processes pixels to provide color, z-depth, and alpha value information. Geometry shader is responsible for processing data at the level of a primitive (triangle, line, and vertex).

Data information from an image is passed from one shader to the next for processing before they are finally output through a frame buffer.

Shaders are also used to incorporate post-processing effects such as Volumetric Lighting, HDR, and Bloom effects to accentuate images in a game.

The language which shaders are programmed in depends on the target environment. For Direct3D, the official language is HLSL. For OpenGL, the official shading language is **OpenGL Shading Language (GLSL)**.

Since most shaders are coded for a GPU, major GPU makers Nvidia and AMD have also tried developing their own languages that can output for both OpenGL and Direct3D shaders. Nvidia developed Cg (deprecated now after version 3.1 in 2012) and AMD developed Mantle (used in some games, such as *Battlefield 4*, that were released in 2014 and seems to be gaining popularity among developers). Apple has also recently released its own shading language known as **Metal Shading Language** for iOS 8 in September 2014 to increase the performance benefits for iOS. Kronos has also announced a next generation graphics API based on OpenGL known as **Vulkan** in early 2015, which appears to be strongly supported by member companies such as Valve Corporation.

The following image is taken from a Direct3D 11 graphics pipeline on MSDN (`http://msdn.microsoft.com/en-us/library/windows/desktop/ff476882(v=vs.85).aspx`). It shows the programmable stages, which data can flow through to generate real-time graphics for our game, known as the rendering pipeline state representation.

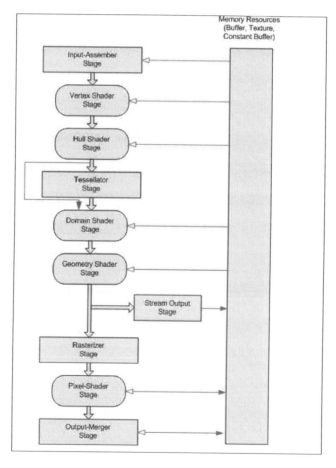

The information here is taken from Microsoft MSDN page. You can use the Direct3D 11API to configure all of the stages. Stages such as vertex, hull, domain, geometry, and pixel-shader (those with the rounded rectangular blocks), are programmable using HLSL. The ability to configure this pipeline programmatically makes it flexible for the game graphics rendering.

What each stage does is explained as follows:

Stage	Function
Input-assembler	This stage supplies data (in the form of triangles, lines, and points) to the pipeline.
Vertex-shader	This stage processes vertices such as undergoing transformations, skinning, and lighting. The number of vertices does not change after undergoing this stage.
Geometry-shader	This stage processes entire geometry primitives such as triangles, lines, and a single vertex for a point.
Stream-output	This stage serves to stream primitive data from the pipeline to memory while on its way to the rasterizer.
Rasterizer	This clips primitives and prepare the primitives for the pixel-shader.
Pixel-shader	Pixel manipulation is done here. Each pixel in the primitive is processed here, for example, pixel color.
Output-merger	This stage combines the various output data (pixel-shader values, depth, and stencil information) with the contents of the render target and depth/stencil buffers to generate the final pipeline result.
Hull-shader, tessellator, and domain-shader	These tessellation stages convert higher-order surfaces to triangles to prepare for rendering.

To help you better visualize what happens in each of the stages, the following image shows a very good illustration of a simplified rendering pipeline for vertices only. The image is taken from an old Cg tutorial. Note that different APIs have different pipelines but rely on similar basic concepts in rendering (source: `http://goanna. cs.rmit.edu.au/~gl/teaching/rtr&3dgp/notes/pipeline.html`).

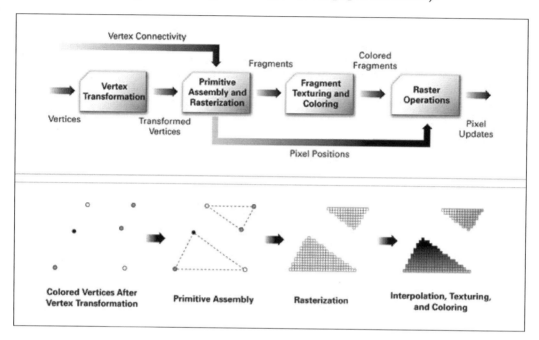

Example flow of how graphics is displayed:

- The CPU sends instructions (compiled shading language programs) and geometry data to the graphics processing unit, located on the graphics card.

- The data is passed through into the vertex shader where vertices are transformed.

- If the geometry shader is active in the GPU, the geometry changes are performed in the scene.

- If a tessellation shader is active in the GPU, the geometries in the scene can be subdivided. The calculated geometry is triangulated (subdivided into triangles).

- Triangles are broken down into fragments. Fragment quads are modified according to the fragment shader.

- To create the feel of depth, the z buffer value is set for the fragments and then sent to the frame buffer for displaying.

APIs – DirectX and OpenGL

Both DirectX and OpenGL are collections of **application programming interfaces** (**APIs**) used for handling multimedia information in a computer. They are the two most common APIs used today for video cards.

DirectX is created by Microsoft to allow multimedia related hardware, such as GPU, to communicate with the Windows system. OpenGL is the open source version that can be used on many operating system including Mac OS.

The decision to use DirectX or OpenGL APIs to program is dependent on operating system of the target machine.

DirectX

Unreal Engine 4 was first launched using DirectX11. Following the announcement that DirectX 12 ships with Windows 10, Unreal has created a DirectX 12 branch from the 4.4 version to allow developers to start creating games using this new DirectX 12.

An easy way to identify APIs that are a part of DirectX is that the names all begin with Direct. For computer games, the APIs that we are most concerned about are Direct3D, which is the graphical API for drawing high performance 3D graphics in games, and DirectSound3D, which is for the sound playback.

DirectX APIs are integral in creating high-performance 2D and 3D graphics for the Windows operating system. For example, DirectX11 is supported in Windows Vista, Windows 7 and Windows 8.1. The latest version of DirectX can be updated through service pack updates. DirectX 12 is known to be shipped with Windows 10.

DirectX12

Direct3D 12 was announced in 2014 and has been vastly revamped from Direct3D 11 to provide significant performance improvement. This is a very good link to a video posted on the MSDN blog that shows the tech demo for DirectX 12: `http://channel9.msdn.com/Blogs/DirectX-Developer-Blog/DirectX-Techdemo`.

(If you are unfamiliar with Direct3D 11 and have not read the *Shaders* section earlier, read that section before proceeding with the rest of the DirectX section.)

Pipeline state representation

If you can recall from the *Shaders* section, we have looked at the programmable pipeline for Direct3D 11. The following image is the same from the *Shaders* section (taken from MSDN) and it shows a series of programmable shaders:

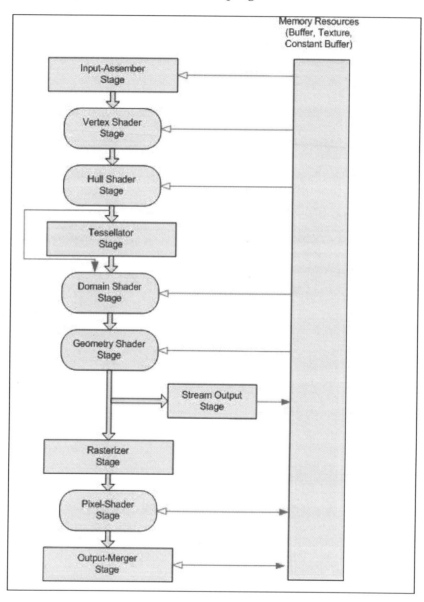

In Direct3D 11, each of the stages is configurable independently and each stage is setting states on the hardware independently. Since many stages have the capability to set the same hardware state due to interdependency, this results in hardware mismatch overhead. The following image is an excellent illustration of how hardware mismatch overhead happens:

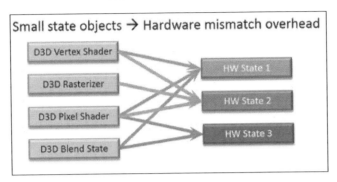

The driver will normally record these states from the application (game) first and wait until the draw time, when it is ready to send it to the display monitor. At draw time, these states are then queried in a control loop before they are is translated into a GPU code for the hardware in order to render the correct scene for the game. This creates an additional overhead to record and query for all the states at draw time.

In Direct3D 12, some programmable stages are grouped to form a single object known as **pipeline state object (PSO)** so that the each hardware state is set only once by the entire group, preventing hardware mismatch overhead. These states can now be used directly, instead of having to spend resources computing the resulting hardware states before the draw call. This reduces the draw call overhead, allowing more draw calls per frame. The PSO that is in use can still be changed dynamically based on whatever hardware native instructions and states that are required.

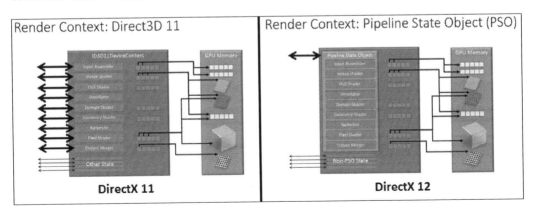

Work submission

In Direct3D 11, work submission to the GPU is immediate. What is new in Direct3D 12 is that it uses command lists and bundles that contain the entire information needed to execute a particular workload.

Immediate work submission in Direct3D 11 means that information is passed as a single stream of command to the GPU and due to the lack of the entire information, these commands are often deferred until the actual work can be done.

When work submission is grouped in the self-contained command list, the drivers can precompute all the necessary GPU commands and then send that list to the GPU, making Direct3D 12 work submission a more efficient process. Additionally, the use of bundles can be thought of as a small list of commands that are grouped to create a particular object. When this object needs to be duplicated on screen, this bundle of commands can be "played back" to create the duplicated object. This further reduces computational time needed in Direct3D 12.

Resource access

In Direct3D 11, the game creates resource views that bind these views to slots at the shaders. These shaders then read the data from these explicit bound slots during a draw call. If the game wants to draw using different resources, it will be done in the next draw call with a different view.

In Direct3D 12, you can create various resource views by using descriptor heaps. Each descriptor heap can be customized to be linked to a specific shader using specific resources. This flexibility to design the descriptor heap allows you to have full control over the resource usage pattern, fully utilizing modern hardware capabilities. You are also able to describe more than one descriptor heap that is indexed to allow easy flexibility to swap heaps, to complete a single draw call.

Lights

We have briefly gone through the types of light in *Chapter 1, An Overview of Unreal Engine*. Let us do a quick recap first. Directional Light emits beams of parallel lights. Point Light emits light like a light bulb (from a single point radially outward in all directions). Spot Light emits light in a conical shape outwards and Sky Light mimics light from the sky downwards on the objects in the level.

In this chapter, we will learn how to use these basic lights to illuminate an interior area. We have already placed a Point Light in *Chapter 2, Creating Your First Level*, and learned how to adjust its intensity to 1700. Here in this chapter, we will learn more about the parameters that we can adjust with each type of light to create the lighting that we want.

Let us first view a level that has been illuminated using these Unreal lights. Load `Chapter4Level_Prebuilt.umap`, build and play the level to look around. Click on the lights that are placed in the level and you will notice that most of lights used are Point or Spot Light. These two forms of lights are quite commonly found in interior lighting.

The next section will guide you to extend the level on your own. Alternatively, you can use the `Chapter4Level_Prebuilt` level to help you along in the creation of your own level since it does take a fair amount of time to create the entire level. If you wish to skip to the next section, feel free to simply use the prebuilt version of the map provided, and go through the other examples in this chapter using the prebuilt map as a reference. However, it will be a great opportunity to revise what you have learned in the previous chapters and extend the level on your own.

Before we embark on the optional exercise to extend the level, let us go through a few tutorial examples on how we can place and configure the different types of light.

Configuring a Point Light with more settings

Open `Chapter4Level.umap` and rename it `Chapter4Level_PointLight.umap`.

Go to **Modes** | **Lights**, drag and drop a Point Light into the level. As Point Light emits light equally in all directions from a single point, **Attenuation Radius**, **Intensity**, and **Color** are the three most common values that are configured for a Point Light.

Attenuation Radius

The following screenshot shows when the Point Light has its default **Attenuation Radius** of **1000**. The radius of the three blue circles is based on the attenuation radius of the Point Light and is used to show its area of effect on the environment.

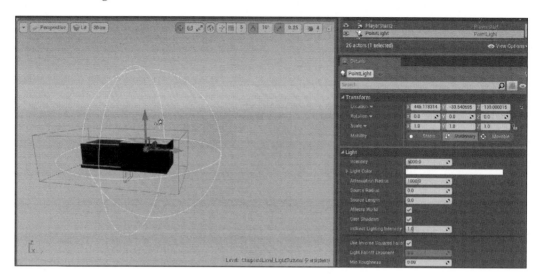

The following screenshot shows when the attenuation radius is reduced to 500. In this situation, you probably cannot see any difference in the lighting since the radius is still larger than the room itself:

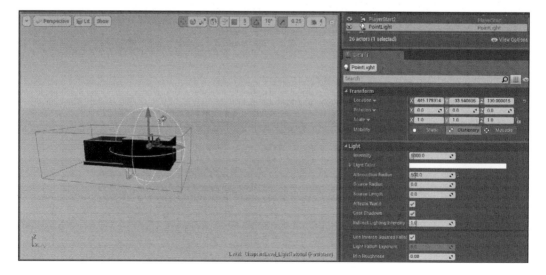

Now, let us take a look at what happens when we adjust the radius much smaller. The following screenshot shows the difference in light brightness when the radius changes. The image on the left is when the attenuation radius is set as 500 and the right when attenuation radius is set as 10.

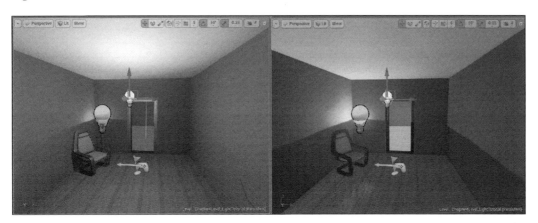

Intensity

Another setting for Point Light is **Intensity**. Intensity affects the brightness of the light. You can play around the Intensity value to adjust the brightness of the light. Before we determine what value to use for this field and how bright we want our light to be, you should be aware of another setting, **Use Inverse Squared Falloff**.

Use Inverse Squared Falloff

Point Lights and Spot Lights have physically based inverse squared falloff set on, as default. This setting is configurable as a checkbox found in the **Light** details under **Advanced**. The following screenshot shows where this property is found in the **Details** panel:

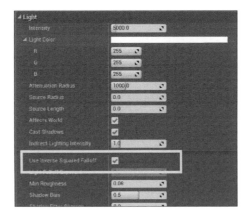

Inverse squared falloff is a physics law that describes how light intensity naturally fades over distance. When we have this setting, the units for intensity use the same units as the lights we have in the real world, in lumens. When inverse squared distance falloff is not used, intensity becomes just a value.

In the previous chapter where we have added our first Point Light, we have set intensity as 1700. This is equivalent to the brightness of a light bulb that has 1700 lumens because inverse squared distance falloff is used.

Color

To adjust the color of Point Light, go to **Light | Color**. The following screenshot shows how the color of the light can be adjusted by specifying the RGB values or using the color picker to select the desired color:

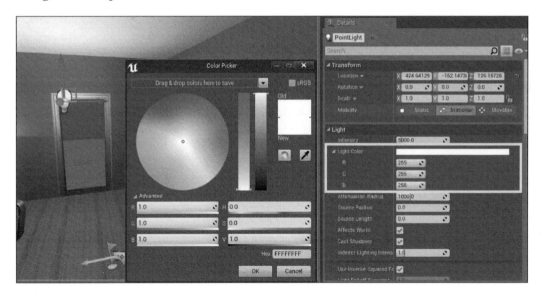

Adding and configuring a Spot Light

Open `Chapter4Level.umap` and rename it `Chapter4Level_SpotLight.umap`. Go to **Modes | Lights**, drag and drop a Spot Light into the level.

The brightness, visible influence radius, and color of a Spot Light can be configured in the same way as the Point Light through the value of **Intensity, Attenuation Radius**, and **Color**.

Since Point Light has light emitting in all directions and a Spot Light emits light from a single point outwards in a conical shape with a direction, the Spot Light has additional properties such as inner cone and outer cone angle, which are configurable.

Inner cone and outer cone angle

The unit for the outer cone angle and inner cone angle is in degrees. The following screenshot shows the light radius that the spotlight has when the outer cone angle = 20 (on the left) and outer cone angle = 15 (on the right). The inner cone angle value did not produce much visible results in the screenshot, so very often the value is 0. However, the inner cone angle can be used to provide light in the center of the cone. This would be more visible for lights with a wider spread and certain IES Profiles.

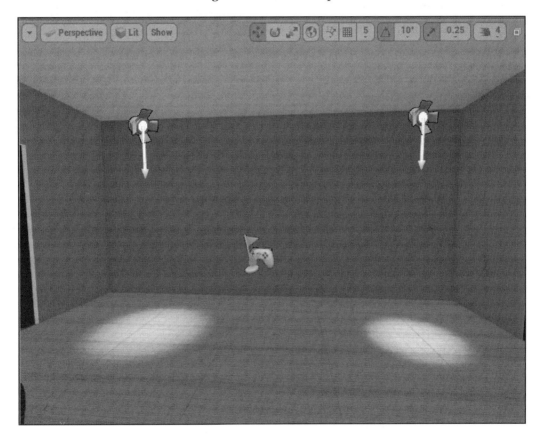

Using the IES Profile

Open `Chapter4Level_PointLight.umap` and rename it `Chapter4Level_IESProfile.umap`.

IES Light Profile is a file that contains information that describes how a light will look. This is created by light manufacturers and can be downloaded from the manufacturers' websites. These profiles could be used in architectural models to render scenes with realistic lighting. In the same way, the IES Profile information can be used in Unreal Engine 4 to render more realistic lights. IES Light Profiles can be applied to a Point Light or a Spot Light.

Downloading IES Light Profiles

IES Light Profiles can be downloaded from light manufacturers' websites. Here's a few that you can use:

- **Cooper Industries**: http://www.cooperindustries.com/content/public/en/lighting/resources/design_center_tools/photometric_tool_box.html
- **Philips**: http://www.usa.lighting.philips.com/connect/tools_literature/photometric_data_1.wpd
- **Lithonia**: http://www.lithonia.com/photometrics.aspx

Importing IES Profiles into the Unreal Engine Editor

From **Content Browser**, click on **Import**, as shown in the following screenshot:

I prefer to have my files in a certain order, hence I have created a new folder called
IESProfile and created subfolders with the names of the manufacturers to better
categorize all the light profiles that were imported.

Using IES Profiles

Continuing from the previous example, select the right Spot Light which we have
in the scene and make sure it is selected. Go to the **Details** panel and scroll down to
show the Light Profile of the light.

Then go to **Content Browser** and go to the IESProfile folder where we have
imported the light profiles into. Click on one of the profiles that you want, drag and
drop it on the IES Texture of the Spot Light. Alternatively, you can select the profile
and go back to the **Details** panel of the **Light** and click on the arrow next to **IES
Texture** to apply the profile on the Spot Light. In the following screenshot, I applied
one of the profiles downloaded from the Panasonic website labeled **144907**.

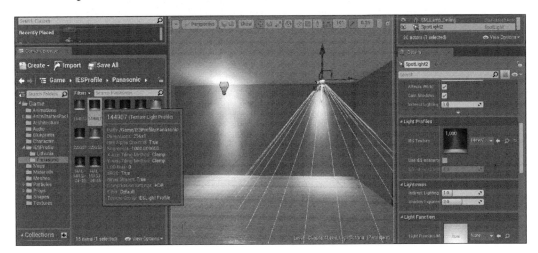

I reconfigured the Spot Light with **Intensity = 1000**, **Attenuation Radius = 1000**,
Outer Cone Angle = 40, and **Inner Cone Angle = 0**.

Next, I deleted the other Spot Light and replaced it with a Point Light where I set **Intensity = 1000** and **Attenuation Radius = 1000**. I also set the **Rotation-Y = -90** and then applied the same IES Profile to it. The following screenshot shows the difference when the same light profile is applied to a Spot Light and a Point Light. Note that the spread of the light in the Spot Light is reduced. This reinforces the concept that a Spot Light provides a conical shaped light with a direction spreading from the point source outwards. The outer cone angle determines this spread. The point light emits light in all directions and equally out, so it did not attenuate the light profile settings allowing the full design of this light profile to be displayed on the screen. This is one thing to keep in mind while using the IES Light Profile and which types of light to use them on.

Adding and configuring a Directional Light

Open Chapter4Level.umap and rename it Chapter4Level_DirectionalLight.umap.

We have already added a Directional Light into our level in *Chapter 2, Creating Your First Level*, and it provides parallel beams of light into the level.

Directional Light can also be used to light the level by controlling the direction of the sun. The screenshot on the left shows the Directional Light when the **Atmosphere Sun Light** checkbox is unchecked. The screenshot on the right shows the Directional Light when the **Atmosphere Sun Light** checkbox is checked. When the **Atmosphere Sun Light** checkbox is checked, you can control the direction of the sunlight by adjusting the rotation of Directional Light.

The following screenshot shows how this looks when **Rotation-Y** = 0. This looks like an early sunset scene:

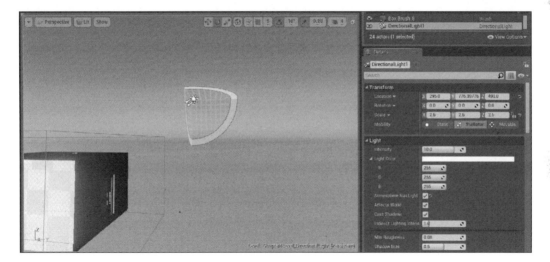

Example – adding and configuring a Sky light

Open `Chapter4Level_DirectionalLight.umap` and rename it `Chapter4Level_Skylight.umap`.

In the previous example, we have added sunlight control in the Directional Light. Build and compile to see how the level now looks.

Now, let us add a Sky Light into the level by going to **Modes | Lights** and then clicking and dragging Sky Light into the level. When adding a Sky Light to the level, always remember to build and compile first in order to see the effect of the Sky Light.

What does a Sky Light do? Sky Light models the color/light from the sky and is used to light up the external areas of the level. So the external areas of the level look more realistic as the color/light is reflecting off the surfaces (instead of using simple white/colored light).

The following screenshot shows the effect of a Sky Light. The left image shows the Sky Light not in the level. The right one shows the Sky Light. Note that the walls now have a tinge of the color of the sky.

Static, stationary, or movable lights

After learning how to place and configure the different lights, we need to consider what kind of lights we need in the level. If you are new to the concept of light, you might want to briefly go through the useful light terms section to help in your understanding.

The following screenshot shows the **Details** panel where you can change a light to be static, stationary, or movable.

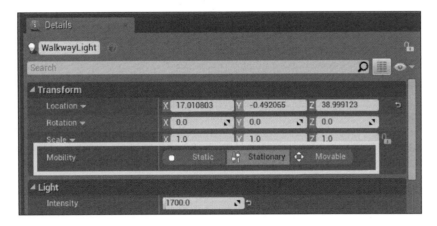

Static and **Stationary** light sounds pretty much similar. What is the difference? When do you want to use a **Static** light and when do you want to use a **Stationary** light?

Common light/shadow definitions

The common light/shadow definitions are as follows:

- **Direct Light**: This is the light that is present in the scene directly due to a light source.

- **Indirect Light**: This is the light in the scene that is not directly from a light source. It is reflected light bouncing around and it comes from all sides.

- **Light Map**: This is a data structure that stores the light/brightness information about an object. This makes the rendering of the object much quicker because we already know its color/brightness information in advance and it is not necessary to compute this during runtime.

- **Shadow Map**: This is a process created to make dynamic shadows. It is fundamentally made up of two passes to create shadows. More passes can be added to render nicer shadows.

Static Light

In a game, we always want to have the best performance, and Static Light will be an excellent option because a Static Light needs only to be precomputed once into a Light Map. So for a Static Light, we have the lowest performance cost but in exchange, we are unable to change how the light looks, move the light, and integrate the effect of this light with moving objects (which means it is unable to create a shadow for the moving object as it moves within the influence of the light) into the environment during gameplay. However, a Static Light can cast shadow on the existing stationary objects that are in the level within its influence of radius. The radius of influence is based on the source radius of the light. In return for low performance cost, a Static Light has quite a bit of limitation. Hence, Static Lights are commonly used in the creation of scenes targeted for devices with low computational power.

Stationary Light

Stationary Light can be used in situations when we do not need to move, rotate, or change the influence radius of the light during gameplay, but allow the light the capacity to change color and brightness. Indirect Light and shadows are prebaked in Light Map in the same way as Static Light. Direct Light shadows are stored within Shadow Maps.

Stationary Light is medium in performance cost as it is able to create static shadow on static objects through the use of distance field shadow maps. Completely dynamic light and shadows is often more than 20 times more intensive.

Movable Light

Movable Light is used to cast dynamic light and shadows for the scene. This should be used sparingly in the level, unless absolutely necessary.

Exercise – extending your game level (optional)

Here are the steps that I have taken to extend the current **Level4** to the prebuilt version of what we have right now. They are by no means the only way to do it. I have simply used a Geometry Brush to extend the level here for simplicity. The following screenshot shows one part of the extended level:

Useful tips

Group items in the same area together when possible and rename the entity to help you identify parts of the level more quickly. These simple extra steps can save time when using the editor to create a mock-up of a game level.

Guidelines

If you plan to extend the game level on your own, open and load `Level4.umap`. Then save map as `Level4_MyPreBuilt.umap`. You can also open a copy of the extended level to copy assets or use it as a quick reference.

Area expansion

We will start by extending the floor area of the level.

Part 1 – lengthening the current walkway

The short walkway was extended to form an L-shaped walkway. The dimensions of the extended portion are X1200 x Y340 x Z40.

BSPs needed	X	Y	Z
Ceiling	1200	400	40
Floor	1200	400	40
Left wall	1570	30	280
Right wall	1260	30	280

Part 2 – creating a big room (living and kitchen area)

The walkway leads to a big room at the end, which is the main living and kitchen area.

BSPs needed	X	Y	Z
Ceiling	2000	1600	40
Floor	2000	1600	40
The left wall dividing the big room and walkway (the wall closest to you as you enter the big room from the walkway)	30	600	340
The light wall dividing the big room and walkway (the wall closest to you as you enter the big room from the walkway)	30	600	340
The left wall of the big room (where the kitchen area is)	1200	30	340
The right wall of the big room (where the dining area is)	2000	30	340
The left wall to the door (the wall across the room as you enter from the walkway, where the window seats are)	30	350	340
The right wall to the door (the wall across the room as you enter from the walkway, where the long benches are)	30	590	340
Door area (consists of brick walls, door frames, and door)			
Wall filler left	30	130	340
Wall filler right	30	126	340
Door x 2	20	116	250
Side door frame x 2	25	4	250
Horizontal door frame	25	242	5
Side brick wall x 2	30	52	340
Horizontal brick wall	30	242	74

Part 3 – creating a small room along the walkway

To create the walkway to the small room, duplicate the same doorframe that we have created in the first room.

BSPs needed	X	Y	Z
Ceiling	800	600	40
Floor	800	600	40
Side wall x 2	30	570	340
Opposite wall (wall with the windows)	740	30	340

Part 4 – Creating a den area in the big room

BSPs needed	X	Y	Z
Sidewall x 2	30	620	340
Wall with shelves	740	30	340

Creating windows and doors

Now that we are done with rooms, we can work on the doors and windows.

Part 1 – creating large glass windows for the dining area

To create the windows, we use a subtractive Geometry Brush to create holes in the wall. First, create one of size X144 x Y30 x Z300 and place it right in the middle between the ceiling and ground. Duplicate this and convert it to an additive brush; adjust the size to X142 x Y4 x Z298.

Apply **M_Metal_Copper** for the frame and **M_Glass** to the addition brush, which was just created. Now, group them and duplicate both the brushes four times to create five windows. The screenshot of the dining area windows is shown as follows:

Part 2 – creating an open window for the window seat

To create the window for the window seat area, create a subtractive geometry brush of size X50 x Y280 x Z220. For this window, we have a protruding ledge of X50 x Y280 x Z5 at the bottom of the window. Then for the glass, we duplicate the subtractive brush of size X4 x Y278 x Z216, convert it to additive brush and adjust it to fit.

Apply **M_Metal_Brushed** for the frame and **M_Glass** to the addition brush that was just created.

Part 3 – creating windows for the room

For the room windows, create a subtractive brush of size X144 x Y40 x Z94. This is to create a hollow in the wall for the prop frame: **SM_WindowFrame**. Duplicate the subtractive brush and prop to create two windows for the room.

Part 4 – creating the main door area

For the main door area, we start by creating the doors and its frame, then the brick walls around the door and lastly, the remaining concrete plain wall.

We have two doors with frames then some brick wall to augment before going back to the usual smooth walls. Here are the dimensions for creating this door area:

BSPs needed	X	Y	Z
Actual door x 2	20	116	250
Side frame x 2	25	4	250
Top frame	25	242	5

Here are the dimensions for creating the area around the door:

BSPs needed	X	Y	Z
Brick wall side x 2	30	52	340
Brick wall top	30	242	74
Smooth wall left	30	126	340
Smooth wall right	30	130	360

Creating basic furniture

Let us begin it part by part as follows.

Part 1 – creating a dining table and placing chairs

For the dining table, we will be customizing a wooden table with a table top of size X480 x Y160 x Z12 and two legs each of size X20 x Y120 x Z70 placed 40 from the edge of the table. Material used to texture is **M_Wood_Walnut**.

Then arrange eight chairs around the table using **SM_Chair** from the `Props` folder.

Part 2 – decorating the sitting area

There are two low tables in the middle and one low long table at the wall. Place three **SM_Couch** from the `Props` folder around the low tables. Here are the dimensions for the larger table:

BSPs needed	X	Y	Z
Square top	140	140	8
Leg x 2	120	12	36

Here are the dimensions for the smaller table:

BSPs needed	X	Y	Z
Leg x 2	120	12	36

Here are the dimensions for a low long table at the wall:

BSPs needed	X	Y	Z
Block	100	550	100

Part 3 – creating the window seat area

Next to the open window, place a geometry box of size X120 x Y310 x Z100. This is to create a simplified seat by the window.

Part 4 – creating the Japanese seating area

The Japanese square table with surface size X200 x Y200 x Z8 and 4 short legs, each of size X20 x Y20 x Z36) is placed close to the corner of the table.

To create a leg space under the table, I used a subtractive brush (X140 x Y140 x Z40) and placed it on the ground under the table. I used the corner of this subtractive brush as a guide as to where to place the short legs for the table.

Part 5 – creating the kitchen cabinet area

This is a simplified block prototype for the kitchen cabinet area. The following are the dimensions for L-shaped area:

BSPs needed	Material	X	Y	Z
Shorter L: cabinet under tabletop	M_Wood_Walnut	140	450	100
Longer L: cabinet under tabletop	M_Wood_Walnut	890	140	100
Shorter L: tabletop	M_Metal_Brushed_Nickel	150	450	10
Longer L: tabletop	M_Metal_Brushed_Nickel	900	150	10
Shorter L: hanging cabinet	M_Wood_Walnut	100	500	100
Longer L: hanging cabinet	M_Wood_Walnut	900	100	100

The following are the dimensions for the island area (hood):

BSPs needed	Material	X	Y	Z
Hood (wooden area)	M_Wood_Walnut	400	75	60
Hood (metallic area)	M_Metal_Chrome	500	150	30

The following are the dimensions for the island area (table):

BSPs needed	Material	X	Y	Z
Cabinet under the table	M_Wood_Walnut	500	150	100
Tabletop	M_Metal_Chrome	550	180	10
Sink (use a subtractive brush)	M_Metal_Chrome	100	80	40
Stovetop	M_Metal_Burnished_Steel	140	100	5

Summary

In this chapter, we covered in-depth information about materials and lights. We learned how the rendering system works and the underlying graphics pipeline/ technology such as Directx 11, DirectX 12, and OpenGL/Vulkan. We also learned how to use the Unreal 4 Material Editor to create custom materials and apply it into your level.

We also explored the different types of lights and adjusting **Intensity, Attenuation Radius,** and other settings to customize lights for the level. We also learned how to import IES light profiles from light manufacturer's website to create realistic lights for the level. We learned about the differences between **Static, Stationary,** and **Movable** lights and how the different lights cast shadows for the level.

In the next chapter, we will learn about animation and artificial intelligence in games. Stay tuned for more!

5
Animation and AI

This chapter is about animation and **artificial intelligence (AI)**.

Animation is what we need in order to see things move in a game. AI is what is required for characters (other than the player) to know how to behave and react while you are in the game.

We will cover the following topics in this chapter:

- Definition of animation
- 3D animation
- Tools required for animation in Unreal Engine 4
- Learning to add animation to your game
- Using an Animation Blueprint
- Learning about Blend Animation
- AI in games
- Designing a **Behavior Tree (BT)**
- Using a Blueprint to implement AI in your game

What is animation?

Animation is the simulation of movement through a series of images or frames.

Before computers came into the picture, animation was created using traditional techniques such as hand-drawn animation and stop-motion animation (or model animation). Hand-drawn animation, as the name suggests, involves hand-drawn scenes on paper. Each scene is repeated on the next sheet of paper with a slight change in the scene. All the papers are put together in sequence and the pages are turned very quickly, like a flipbook. The slight changes on the sheets of paper create 2D animation, and this can be filmed into a motion film. This technique is used very often in Disney cartoons and movies. As you can imagine, this is a very time-consuming way to produce animation, as you would need thousands of drawings to create seconds of the film.

Stop-motion animation involves creating models, moving them a little in each frame to mimic movement, and filming this sequence to construct an entire scene. The tedious process of capturing countless snippets has limited the use of this method in favor of more mainstream animation techniques today.

Computer animation is quite similar to stop-motion animation as computer graphics is moved a little in each frame; these frames are then rendered on screen. For computer games, we use computer animation by creating 3D models using tools, such as Maya and 3ds Max. Then, we animate these models to simulate life-like behavior and actions for the game. Animation is needed for all things in order to make them move. Characters need to be animated so that they can look real—they can be in an idle position, walk, run, or execute any other action that needs to be performed in the course of the game.

Motion capture is also another very popular way to animate characters these days. This technology basically uses recorded human actions to create the computer graphic character's behavior. If you have watched the movie *Avatar*, the blue avatar characters were, in fact, played by human actors and then enhanced to look the way they did using computer graphics. For the filming of the movie, they advanced the motion capture technology into what is now called **performance capture**. This advancement in technology has empowered film and game makers to capture the details in animation in such a way that can make a CG character stand out.

Understanding how to animate a 3D model

Although the objective of this book is not to teach you how to animate a model, it is important to understand how animation is done so that you can understand better how to get game characters in a game to move and behave according to design.

As mentioned earlier, we can animate 3D models using tools, such as Maya or 3ds Max. We can then record their changes and then render these animations on screen when needed.

Preparing before animation

In game development, the creation of animation falls under the responsibility of an animator. Before an animation can be first created, we need to first have a 3D model that's been created by a 3D modeler. The 3D modeler is responsible for giving the object its shape and texturing it. Depending on the type of object we're dealing with, the exact process to get an object properly rigged can be slightly different. Rigging needs to be done before handing over the object to the animator to create specific animations. Sometimes, animators also need to fine-tune the rigs for better control of the animation.

Rigging is a process where a skeleton is placed in the mesh and joints that are created for the skeleton. The collection of bones/joints is known as the **rig**. The rig provides control points, which the animator can use to move the object in order to create the desired animation. I will use a human character model in my explanation here so that you can understand this concept easily.

The 3D or character modeler first shows how the face and body of a model are shaped. It then determines how tall the model is, creates all the required features by adding primitives to the model, and then textures it to give color to its eyes, hair, and so on. The model is now ready but still jelly on the inside because we have not given it any internal structure. Rigging is the process where we add bones to the body to hold it up. The arm can be rotated because we have given it a shoulder bone (scapula), arm bone (humerus), and a joint that can mimic the ball and socket joint. The joint we have in place for rigging is made up of a group of constraints that limit movement in various planes and angles. Hierarchies are also applied to the bone structure to help the bones link each other. The fingers are linked to the hand, which is linked to the arm. Such a relationship can be put in place so that movement looks real when one of parts moves and the rest of the parts naturally move together as well.

Tools, such as Maya and 3ds Max, provide some simplification to the rigging process, as you can use standard rigs as the base, and tweak this base according to the needs of the model. Some models are taller and require longer bones. A 3D model must have a simple skeletal structure that adheres closely to the shape and size of a 3D model. Similar sized 3D models can share the same skeletal structure.

To better understand how we can add animation to our game levels, let's learn how computer animation is created and how we can make these models move.

How is animation created?

Animation basically mimics how life moves in the real world. Many companies go to great lengths to make computer animation as accurate as possible through the use of motion capture. They film actual movements in real life and then recreate these movements using computer 3D models.

When creating animations, the animator makes use of the bones and joints created during the rigging process and adjusts them in place using as much detail as possible to mimic their natural movement. The joints and bones work together to affect the body posture. These movements are then recorded as short animation clips known as an animation sequence. Animation sequences form the most basic blocks of animation, and they can be played once or repeatedly to create an action. For example, a walking animation is only 1.8 seconds long but can be replayed over and over to simulate walking. When this sequence is repeated again, it is commonly known as an animation loop.

Animation sequences can also be linked to form a chain of actions. While transitioning from one sequence to another, some blending might be needed in order for the movement to look natural.

What Unreal Engine 4 offers for animation in games

Animation in Unreal Engine 4 is mostly done in the Persona editor. This editor offers four different modes: **Skeleton**, **Mesh**, **Animation**, and **Graph**. These modes mainly exist so that you can jump straight into one of them to edit/create the animations more effectively. So, they are simply a loose group of functions that can be used to control the different aspects of animation. We will learn how to make use of the functions in Persona to add animation to our level.

To help improve team collaboration, Unreal Engine 4 also released a previously in-house-only toolset, which is a plugin for Maya (compatible for Maya 2013 and higher versions), known as **Animation and Rigging Toolset (ART)**. This toolset provides a user interface to allow the creation of a skeleton, placement of the skeleton, and rig creation within Maya itself. We will not go into the details of this toolset, but you can find more information on this in Unreal's online documentation at `https://docs.unrealengine.com/latest/INT/Engine/Content/Tools/MayaRiggingTool/index.html`.

Importing animation from Maya/3ds Max

As many artists use Maya and 3ds Max to create 3D models and animation, Unreal Engine 4 has a great FBX Import pipeline that allows you to successfully import skeletal models, animation sequences, and morph targets. This makes it easy to transfer assets to the Unreal Editor and put them into the game. Unreal also tries to stabilize the import of art assets from other software, such as Blender and MODO.

Tutorial – importing the animation pack from Marketplace

Since 3D models and animation are first created outside Unreal Engine, for the purpose of learning about how animation works, we will import an animation pack that contains a 3D model with a number of animation sequences first, and we'll then learn how to make use of the different tools in the Unreal Editor for animation.

Unreal Engine offers a number of downloadable packs in Marketplace. Marketplace is in the start menu screen, which is under the **Launch** button. The following screenshot shows the startup screen that has the **Marketplace** tab selected for the downloadable packs. Search for **Animation Starter Pack** in Marketplace under **Characters and Animations**. This particular pack is free to download. Click on **Animation Started Pack** to download it.

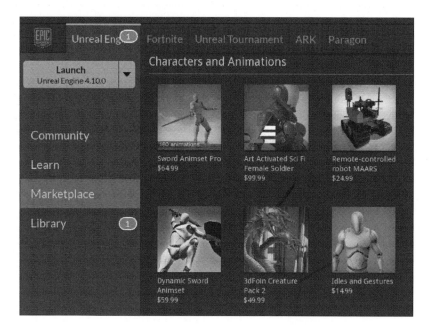

After the pack is downloaded, you will find the pack added to the **Library**. The following screenshot shows where **Animator Starter Pack** is found in **Library** under **Vault**:

Now that we have the **Animation Starter Pack** in our **Library**, we can add it to our current project and start playing with the animations.

Click on **Add To Project** and a pop-up screen with all the current projects that are present in Unreal Engine will appear. Select the name of the project that you have been creating for all the various levels and all the tutorial examples. If you have followed the same project and level naming convention as me, it will be `MyProject`. I have also opened `Chapter4Level` from the previous chapter and renamed it `Chapter5Level`. The following screenshot shows `AnimStarterPack` loaded in the project:

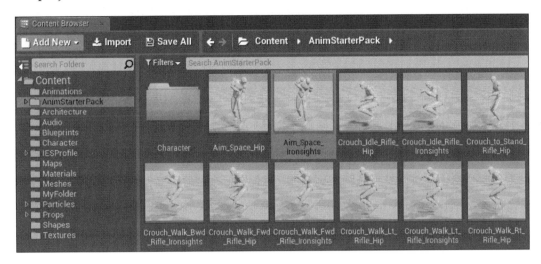

What can you do with Persona?

Persona gives game developers the ability to playback and preview animation sequences, combine animation sequences into a single animation by blending, creating montages, editing skeletons/sockets, and controlling animation with Blueprints. I hope you still remember what you have learned about Blueprints in *Chapter 3*, *Game Object – More and Move*.

Tutorial – assigning existing animation to a Pawn

After adding the free animation pack into your project in the previous exercise, it is time to add some animation to the level. First of all, open `Chapter4Level`, rename it `Chapter5Level`, and then navigate to the `AnimStarterPack` folder using **Content Browser**. Go to the `Character` subfolder and click and drag **HeroTPP** into the level.

This screenshot shows how **HeroTPP** is added to the level:

The **HeroTPP** looks fake and frozen, right? Now, let's give him a better pose. Click on **HeroTPP** to display the details. Go to the **Animation** tab under **Details** and input the **Animation Mode** settings. Use **Animation Asset**, navigate and click on **Jog_Fwd_Rifle** in `AnimStarterPack` (in **Content Browser**), and then click on the arrow next to **Anim to Play**.

Here is a zoomed-in view of the **Animation** settings:

Now, build and play the level. You will see the character that you have just added to the level, is jogging.

This is the straightforward way to animate a character. However, the character continues to loop through this animation no matter what is happening around. We probably want the character to be able to react to the environment and conditions of the game. So, how can we do this?

Why do we need to blend animations?

In the previous exercise, we learned how to make a skeletal mesh take on a single animation. But can we make the skeletal mesh start running in a straight line? The next few sections of animation exercises will explain how we can do this and, subsequently, add more to this basic animation.

First of all, you need to remember that animation sequences/poses are played when you tell them to. While animating character, you need to look into the details so that the character looks normal.

Now, let's quickly recap what we did in the previous exercise: the skeletal mesh character was a zombie with no animation attached. When we linked the run animation and set it to play, the character immediately seemed like it was running. So, if we want the character to stop running, we can remove the run animation. The character goes back to looking like a zombie that hasn't been animated. If we did this in a game, you would probably think that there is something very wrong with the animation. Zombie->Running->Zombie. Nothing realistic about it.

How can we improve this? We start with an idle pose for the character; an idle pose is one where the character stands at a fixed spot and breathes. Breathing is part of animation too. It makes the character look like it's alive. Next, we set it to play the run animation. To stop this animation, we allow the character to take the idle position again. Not a bad attempt for this iteration. The character doesn't look like a zombie now, but it looks and feels real.

What else can we do to make this even better? Let's use an analogy of someone driving a car normally (not a race car driver). When moving from the start position, you accelerate from a speed of 0 up to a comfortable cruising speed. When you want to stop, you reduce the cruising speed by stepping on the brakes and then gradually go back to 0 (to avoid a stopping suddenly and giving your passengers the unpleasant experience of being thrown forward). Similarly, we can use this to help us design our character's transition from a stationary position. We will use a tool called **Blend Animation** to create this transition so that we can make the movement of the character a little more realistic.

Blend Animation, as the name suggests, blends various types of animation using variables. It can be a simple one-dimensional relationship where we use speed as an axis to blend the animations or a two-dimensional relationship where we use both speed and direction to blend animations. Unreal Engine's Blend Animation tool is capable of setting up the blending of animations in different ways.

Tutorial – creating a Blend Animation

In this example, we will use speed as the parameter to blend the animation. Let's quickly cover the thought process here first before listing the steps to follow in the Unreal Editor to achieve this. This would help in your understanding of how this process works instead of simply following the process to make something happen.

At speed = 0, we assign the idle pose. As the speed increases, we should switch the animation from an idle to a walking animation. As the speed increases even more, the animation switches from walking to jogging, and then running. Here's an illustration of how the blend would look:

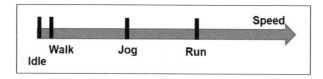

Next, let's identify which animation sequences we have in the animation pack and would be suitable for each of the stages:

- **Idle_Rifle_Hip**
- **Walk_Fwd_Rifle_Ironsights**
- **Jog_Fwd_Rifle**
- **Sprint_Fwd_Rifle**

To create a simple 1D Blend Space, we can right-click on the `Character` folder, and go to **Create Asset | Animation | Blend Space 1D**. Alternatively, you can select the `Character` folder in **Content Browser**, click on the **Create** button at the top, go to **Animation**, and then **Blend Space 1D**.

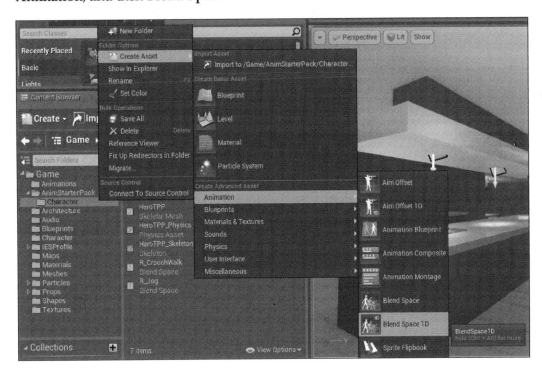

Select **HeroTPP_Skeleton**; clicking on this creates a new Blend Space 1D. Rename **newblendspace1d** to WalkJogRun. Double-click on the newly created **WalkJogRun** to open the editor. This will propel you straight to the **Animation** tab of the editor. Notice that this part is highlighted in the following screenshot. In the **SkeletonMesh** field, we have **HeroTPP_Skeleton**, which was what we selected when creating the blend space earlier.

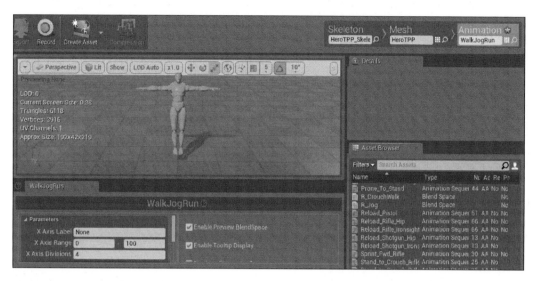

In the **Animation** editor, you have access to **Asset Browser** (which is, by default, in the bottom right-hand side of the screen). Clicking on the animation assets will allow you to preview how the animation looks.

Let's first set the **X Axis Label** to Speed. **X Axis Range** is from 0 to 375. Leave **X Axis Divisions** as **4**.

The number of divisions creates segments in the speed graph that we have. Based on what we selected earlier for the Idle, Walk, Jog, and Run states, find the animation using **Asset Browser**, click and drop the animation into the **WalkJogRun** tab into the appropriate sections, as shown in the following screenshot:

Idle_Rifle_Hip is at speed = 0. Set **Walk_Fwd_Rifle_Ironsights** in the first division line. When you drag an animation into the graph, it creates a node and snaps at one of the division lines. Set **Jog_Fwd_Rifle** in the second division line and set **Sprint_Fwd_Rifle** at speed = 375. To preview how the animation blends, move the mouse over the graph along the vertical axis.

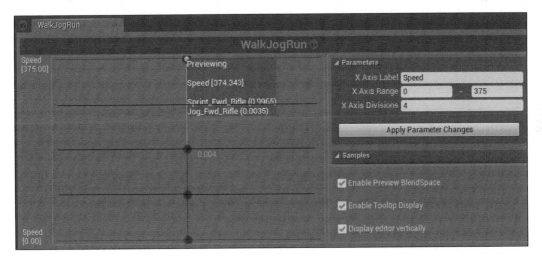

Tutorial – setting up the Animation Blueprint to use a Blend Animation

Now we have created a Blend Animation that uses speed as a parameter. How do we make an NPC change speed and then link this animation to it so that as the speed changes and the animation that is played also changes?

For a simple implementation of getting the speed and animation to change, we will set up the Animation Blueprint. Go to **Content Browser**. Navigate to **Animation | Character**; then, navigate and click on **Create Asset | Animation | Animation Blueprint**:

Upon selecting **Animation Blueprint**, the editor will prompt you about the base class that you want the Animation Blueprint to be created in. This screenshot shows the options that are available for selection:

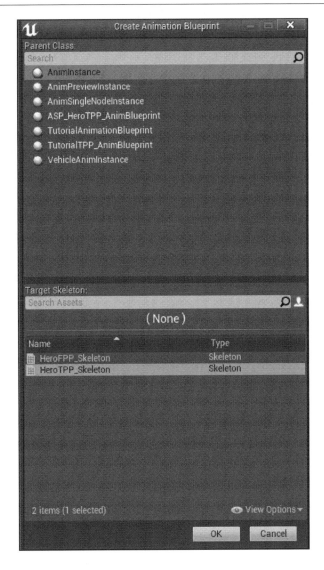

In this example, we will pick the most basic generic class, AnimInstance, to build our Animation Blueprint in. Select **HeroTPP_Skeleton** as the target skeletal mesh for this blueprint. Name this Animation Blueprint MyNPC_Blueprint.

To check whether you have selected the correct target skeletal mesh, look in the **Skeleton** tab in the **Blueprint** window, as shown in the following screenshot. You should see **HeroTPP_Skeleton** in the box. The screenshot also shows the **Graph** tab that's been selected with the empty default AnimGraph showing. We will proceed through this exercise with the **Graph** tab selected, unless specified otherwise.

AnimGraph

This screenshot shows the default blank AnimGraph. **Final Animation Pose** will receive the output of the skeletal mesh that's been specified:

First, we want to add a state machine by right-clicking within the AnimGraph and navigating to **State Machines | Add New State Machine...**, as shown in the following screenshot:

Rename the newly created state machine **Movement**:

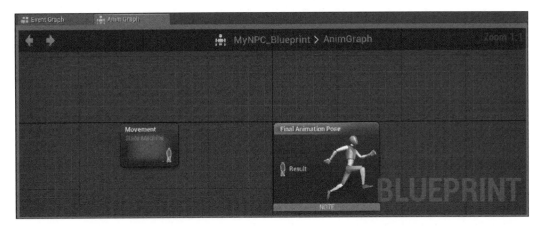

Double-click on **Movement**. Create a new state named **WalkJogRun**:

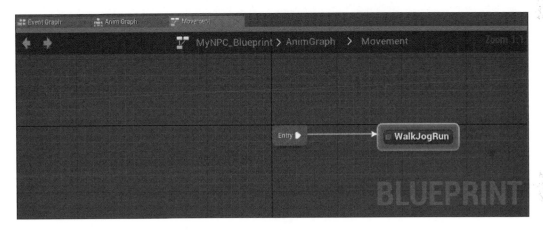

Double-click on the newly created **WalkJogRun** state to modify the state in a new tab. Go to the **Asset Browser** tab, look for **WalkJogRun** blendspace, which we created in the previous exercise, and click and drag it into the editor. Link **WalkJogRun** blendspace to the final animation, as shown in the following screenshot. Notice that speed = 0.00 is specified in the blendspace node; this was the variable that we defined to control the change of the animation when we created blendspace in the earlier exercise.

Next, we need to create a variable so that we can pass in a value to the **WalkJogRun** blendspace speed variable. To do so, we need to click and drag the green dot next to the **Speed** on the blendspace node to open up a contextual menu, look for **Promote to Variable**, and then click on it. This promotes speed in the blendspace node to a float variable, which we would set to control the speed and type of animation that will be played. Rename this new variable **Speed**. The following screenshot shows how we have created and connected a **Speed** variable to **WalkJogRun** blendspace, which is linked to **Final Animation Pose**:

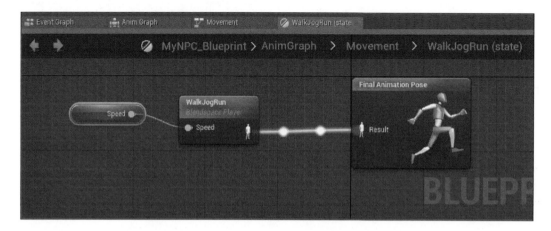

Now, go back to link **Movement** to **Final Animation Pose**:

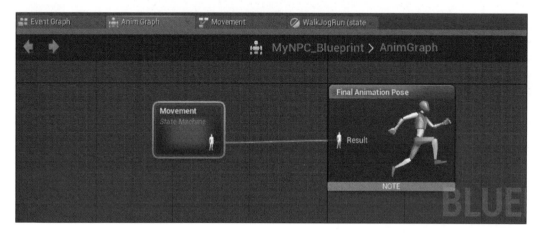

Now, the entire AnimGraph is linked up. Click on **Compile**, and you would see the preview of the character model updated, as shown in the following screenshot. The white moving dots show how data flows through the system. The speed is 0 here.

We can also use this tab to see live preview as we change the value to **Speed**. The following screenshot shows you when speed is 50. The character model assumes a walking pose.

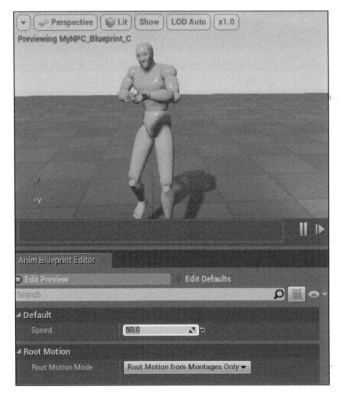

Through AnimGraph, we were able to set up **Speed** as a variable and link this variable to **WalkJogRun** blendspace, which, in turn, controls what animation to play at which speed. We need to now think about how to provide some logic to determine how the speed of the NPC changes.

EventGraph

EventGraph is used to program logic into the Blueprint.

In this example, we will use EventGraph to create logic to change the speed values that will, in turn, affect the NPC's animation control.

To create a more complex intelligent decision-making process, which is termed as AI, we will need to use a set of AI-related nodes in EventGraph. We will learn more about creating AI in the next section.

The following screenshot shows the default new **EventGraph** tab in the Animation Blueprint.

The **Event Blueprint Update Animation** node can be thought of as the source that sends a pulse through the EventGraph network. As this pulse travels through the network, it goes through a series of questions that you design to determine which animation is played.

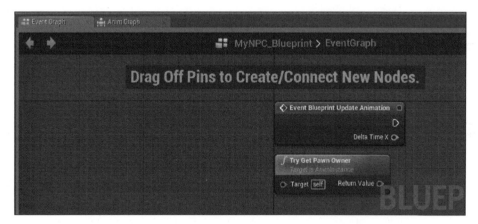

Try Get Pawn Owner is to get the owner that Animation Blueprint is assigned to. This is simply used in combination with another node, **IsValid**, to ensure that we have a valid owner before setting values to change the animation.

To make **MyNPC_Blueprint** work for the **Hero_TPP** mesh that we have in the level, we will need to first delete the **Try Get Pawn Owner** node and replace it with **Get Owning Component**. Right-click on the EventGraph and type Get. In the contextual menu that is opened, scroll down to find **Get Owning Component**. This screenshot shows where the **Get Owning Component** node is:

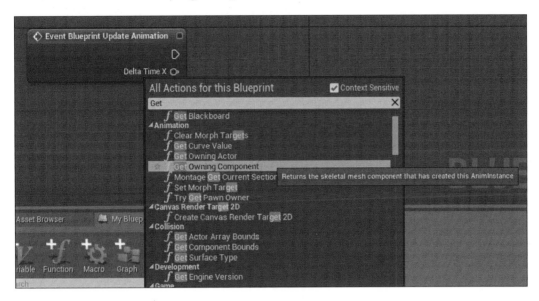

In the same way, right-click in the editor and type IsValid to look for the node. This screenshot shows where to get the **IsValid** node:

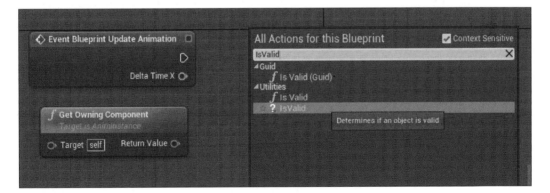

Now, link the triangular output from **Event Blueprint Update Animation** to the **Exec** input of the **IsValid** node (which is also a triangular input). Link **Return Value** (this has a blue circle next to it) output from **Get Owning Component** to **Input Object** (this has a blue circle next to it) of the **IsValid** node. The following screenshot shows the linkage of the three nodes.

The explanation for this is that at every tick, we need to check whether the target skeleton mesh is valid.

For now, let's simply set the speed of the NPC to 100 if the target skeleton mesh is valid. So, right-click on the EventGraph area, and type SetSpeed to filter the options. Click and select **Set Speed**, as shown in this screenshot:

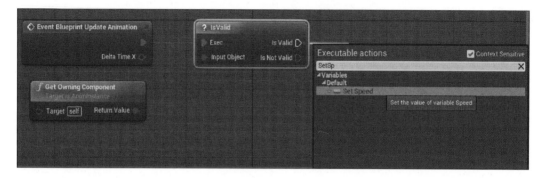

Link the **Is Valid** output of the **IsValid** node to the input (this has a triangular symbol) of the **SET Speed** node. Then, click on the box next to **Speed** and type 100 to set the speed:

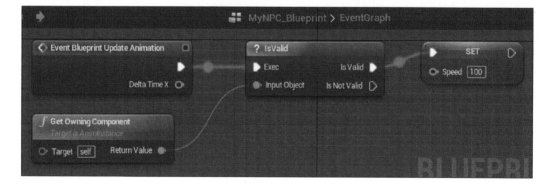

Save and recompile now to see how the preview model changes. The following screenshot shows the model playing the walk animation when speed is set to 100:

Now, Animation Blueprint is ready for use in the game level. We need to assign this Animation Blueprint to a character in the game. Save and close the Animation Blueprint editor to go back to the main editor.

To assign the Blueprint to the skeleton mesh, we will click on the existing **HeroTPP** to display the details panel. Focus on the animation part of the panel; the following screenshot shows the original setting that I have when there is no animation sequence linked to the skeleton mesh and it does not use an Animation Blueprint. Set **Animation Mode** to **Use Animation Asset** and **Anim to Play** to **None**:

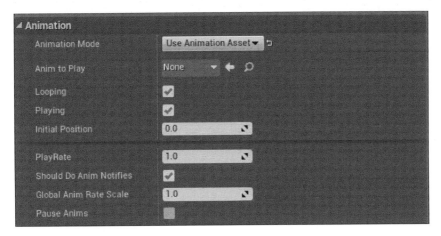

To use **MyNPC_Blueprint** for this skeleton mesh, set **Animation Mode** to **Use Animation Blueprint**. Select **MyNPC_Blueprint** for **Anim Blueprint Generated Class**:

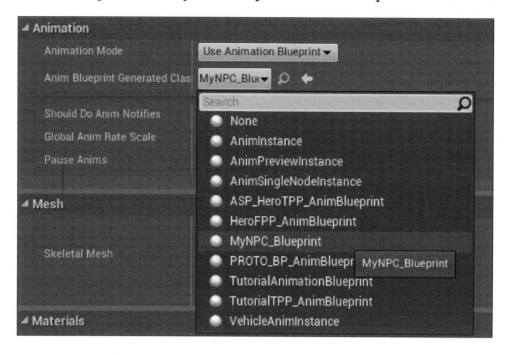

Now, compile and run the game; you would see the NPC walking on the same spot with the speed set as 100.

Artificial intelligence

AI is a decision-making process that adds NPCs in a game. AI is a programmable decision-making process for NPCs to govern their responses and behaviors in a game. A game character that is not controlled by a human player has no form of intelligence, and when these characters need to have a higher form of decision-making process, we apply AI to them.

AI in games has progressed tremendously over the years and NPCs can be programmed to behave in a certain way, sometimes, with some form of randomness, making it almost unpredictable so that players do not have a simple, straightforward strategy to win the level.

The decision-making process, which is also the logic of the NPCs, is stored in a data structure known as a Behavior Tree. We will first learn how to design a simple Behavior Tree then learn how to implement this in Unreal Engine 4.

Understanding a Behavior Tree

Learning how to design a good decision-making tree is very important. This is the foundation on which programmers or scripters rely to create the behavior of a character in a game. The Behavior Tree is the equivalent of a construction blueprint for architects who design your house.

A Behavior Tree has roots that branch out into layers of child nodes, which are ordered from left to right (this means that you always start from the left-most node when traversing the child nodes) that describe the decision-making process. The nodes that make up the Behavior Tree mainly fall into three categories: Composite, Decorator, or Leaf. Once you are familiar with a couple of the common types of nodes in each of the three categories, you would be ready to create your own complex behaviors:

	Composite	Decorator	Leaf
Children nodes	Having one or more children are possible.	This can only have a single child node.	This cannot have any children at all.
Function	Children nodes are processed, depending on the particular type of composite node.	This either transforms results from a child node's status, terminates the child, or repeats the processing of the child, depending on the particular type of Decorator.	This executes specific game actions/tasks or tests.
Node examples	The **Sequence** node processes the children nodes from the left-most child in sequence, collects results from each child, and passes the overall success or failure result over to the parent (note that even when only one child fails and the rest succeed, the overall result is failure). This can be thought of as an **AND** node.	The **Inverter** node converts a success to a failure and pass this inverted result back to the parent. It works vice versa as well.	The **Shoot Once leaf** node shows that the NPC would shoot once and return a success or failure, depending on the result.

Exercise – designing the logic of a Behavior Tree

This is a simple walkthrough of how a Behavior Tree can be constructed. The following legend will help you identify the different components of a Behavior Tree:

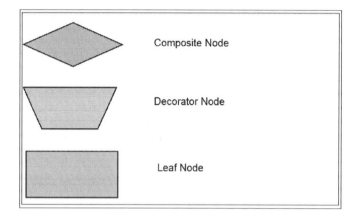

Example – creating a simple Behavior Tree

The following figure shows a simple response for an enemy NPC. The enemy will only start attacking when the war starts.

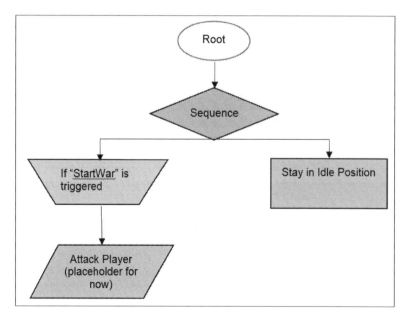

The following figure has been expanded on the earlier Behavior Tree. It gives a more detailed description of how the enemy NPC should approach the target. The NPC will run towards the target (the player character in this case), and if it is close enough, it starts shooting the player.

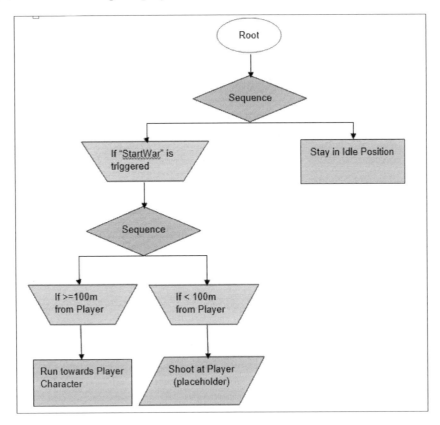

Next, we set more behaviors that show how the NPC will shoot the player. We give the enemy NPC a little intelligence: hide if someone is shooting at it and start shooting if no one is shooting at it; if the player starts moving in toward it, the NPC starts moving backward to a better spot or goes for a death match (it shoots the player at close range).

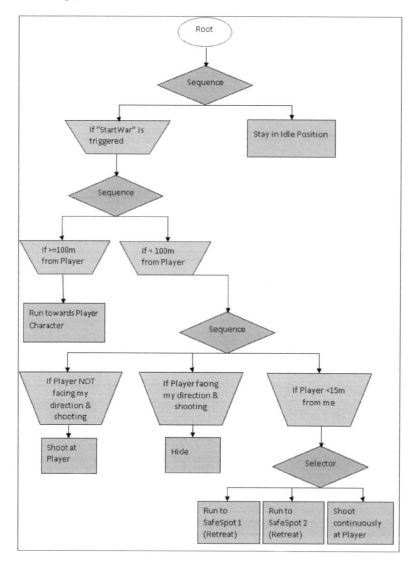

How to implement a Behavior Tree in Unreal Engine 4

The Unreal Editor allows complex Behavior Trees to be designed using the visual scripting Blueprints together with several AI components.

There is also an option in Unreal Engine 4 where very complex AI behaviors can be programmed in the conventional way or in combination with Blueprint visual scripting.

The nodes for BT in UE4 are broadly divided into five categories. Just to recap, we have already learned a little about the first four in the previous section; **Service** is the only new category here:

- **Root**: The starting node for a Behavior Tree and every Behavior Tree has only one root.

- **Composite**: These are the nodes that define the root of a branch and the base rules for how this branch is executed.

- **Decorator**: This is also known as a **conditional**. These attach themselves to another node and make decisions on whether or not a branch in the tree, or even a single node, can be executed.

- **Task**: This is also known as a Leaf in a typical BT. These are the leaves of the tree, that is, the nodes that "do" things.

- **Service**: These are attachments to composite nodes. They are executed at a defined frequency, as long as their branch is being executed. These are often used to make checks and update the **Blackboard**. These take the place of traditional parallel nodes in other Behavior Tree systems.

Navigation Mesh

For AI characters to move around in the game level, we need to specifically tell the AI character which areas in the map are accessible.

Unreal Engine has implemented a mesh-like component known as **Navigation Mesh**. The Navigation Mesh is pretty much like a block volume; you could scale the size of the mesh to cover a specific area in the game level that an AI character can move around in. This limits the area in which an AI can go and makes the movement of the character more predictable.

Tutorial – creating a Navigation Mesh

Go to **Modes** | **Volumes**. Click and drop **Nav Mesh Bounds Volume** into your game level. The following screenshot shows where you can find **Nav Mesh Bounds Volume** in the editor:

If you are unable to see **Nav Mesh Bounds Volume** in your map, go to the **Show** settings within the editor, as shown in the following screenshot. Make sure the checkbox next to **Navigation** is checked:

Scale and move the Navigation Mesh to cover the area of the floor you want the AI character to be able to access. What I have done in the following screenshot is to scale the mesh to fit the floor area which I want my AI character to walk in. Translate the mesh upward and downward to allow it to be slightly above the actual ground mesh. The Navigation Mesh should sort of enclose the ground mesh. This screenshot shows how the mesh looks when it is visible:

Tutorial – setting up AI logic

Here's an overview of the components that we will create for this tutorial:

- Blueprint AIController (**MyNPC_AIController**)
- Blueprint Character (**MyNPC_Character**)
- BlackBoard (**MyNPC_Brain**)
- Behavior Tree (**MyNPC_BT**)
- Blueprint Behavior Tree Task (**Task_PickTargetLocation**)

The important takeaway from this tutorial is to learn how the components are linked up to work together to create logic; we make use of this logic to control the behavior of the NPC.

In terms of file structure in **Content Browser** for these different file types, you can group the different components into different folders. For this example, since we are only creating one NPC character with logic, I will put all these components into a single folder for simplicity. I created `MyFolder` under the main directory for this purpose.

We start creating the AI logic of our NPC starting with AIController and Character. The Character Blueprint is the object that contains the link to the mesh, and we will drag and drop this Character Blueprint into the level map after we make some initial configurations. The AIController is the component that gives the NPC character its logic.

We will discuss the rest of the other three components as we go along.

Creating the Blueprint AIController

Go to **Create | Blueprint**. Type in `AIController` into the textbox to filter by class, as shown in the following screenshot. Select **AIController** as the parent class.

Rename this AIController Blueprint as `MyNPC_AIController`:

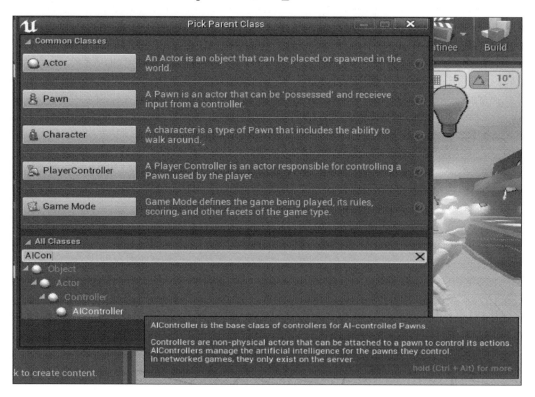

We will come back to configure this later.

Creating the Blueprint character

Go to **Create | Blueprint**, and type in `Character` in the textbox to filter by class. Select **Character** as the parent class for the Blueprint, as shown in the following screenshot. Rename this Blueprint as `MyNPC_Character`.

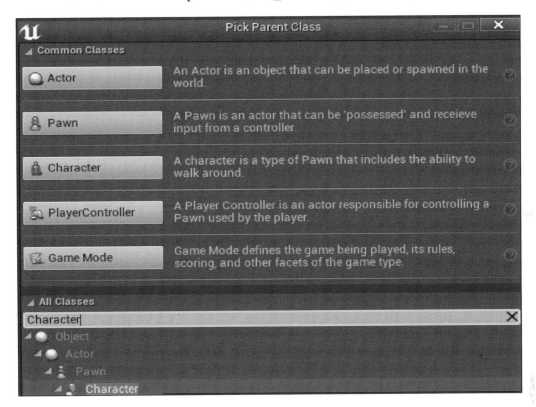

Adding and configuring Mesh to a Character Blueprint

Double-click on **MyNPC_Character** in **Content Browser** to open the Character Blueprint editor. Go to the **Components** tab.

In the **Perspective** space view, you will see an empty wireframe-capsule-shaped object, as shown in the following screenshot. In the **Details** panel in the Blueprint editor, scroll to the **Mesh** section, and we will add a mesh to this Blueprint by selecting an existing mesh we have. You can go to **Content Browser**, select **HeroTPP**, and click on the arrow next to it. Alternatively, you can click on the search button next to the box and find **HeroTPP**:

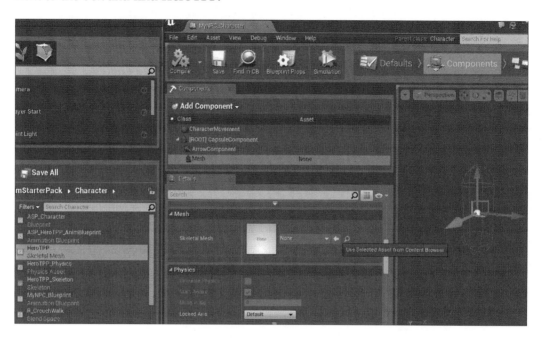

After selecting **HeroTPP** as the skeletal mesh, you will see the mesh appearing in the wireframe capsule. Notice that the **HeroTPP** skeletal mesh is much larger than the capsule wireframe, as shown in the following screenshot. We want to be able to adjust the size of the wireframe to surround the height and width of the skeletal mesh as closely as possible. This will define the collision volume of the character.

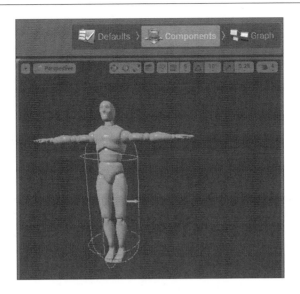

This figure shows when the wireframe for the skeletal mesh is the correct height:

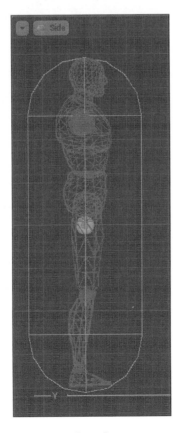

Linking AIController to the Character Blueprint

Go to the **Default** tab of **MyNPC_Character**, scroll to the AI section, and click on the scroll box to display the options available for AIControllers. Select **MyNPC_AIController** to assign the character to use this AIController, as shown in this screenshot. Compile, save, and close **MyNPC_Character** for now.

Go to **Content Browser**, and click and drop **MyNPC_Character** into the level map. Compile and play the level. You will see that the character appears in the level but it is static.

Adding basic animation

Similar to the early implementation of assigning an animation to the mesh, we will add animation to **MyNPC_Character**. Double-click on **MyNPC_Character** to open the editor. Go the **Default** tab, scroll to the **Animation** section, and assign the Animation Blueprint (**MyNPC_Blueprint**), which we created earlier for this Character Blueprint. The following screenshot shows how we can assign animation to the character. Compile and save **MyNPC_Character**:

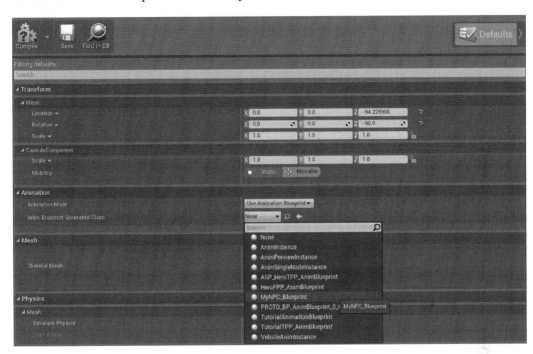

Now, play the level again, and you will see that the character is now walking on the spot (as we have set the speed to 100 in the Animation Blueprint, **MyNPC_Blueprint**).

Configuring AIController

Go to **Content Browser**. Then, go to **MyFolder** and double-click on **MyNPC_ AIController** to open the editor. We will now add nodes in EventGraph to design the logic.

Our first mission is to get the character to move forward (instead of just walking on the same spot).

Nodes to add in EventGraph

The following are the nodes to be added in EventGraph:

- **Event Tick**: This is used to trigger the loop to run at every tick
- **Get Controlled Pawn**: This returns the pawn of AIController (which will be the pawn of **HeroTPP**)
- **Get Actor Forward Vector**: This gets the forward vector
- **Add Movement Input**: This links the target to **Get Controlled Pawn** and **Link World Direction** to the output of **Get Actor Forward Vector**
- **IsValid**: This is to ensure that the pawn exists first before actually changing the pawn values

The following screenshot shows the final EventGraph that we want to create:

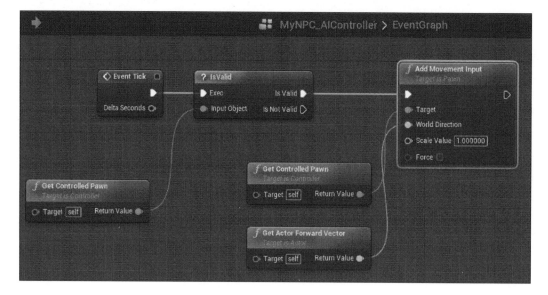

Now, play the level again, and you will see that the character is now walking forward. But it's doing this a little too quickly. We want to adjust the maximum speed at which the character moves.

Adjusting movement speed

Double-click on **MyNPC_Character** to open the editor. Go to the **Default** tab, scroll to the **Character Movement** section, and set **Max Walk Speed** to **100**, as shown in this screenshot:

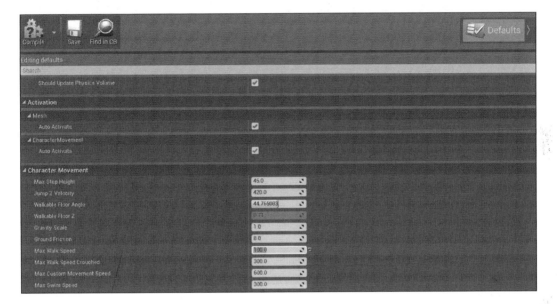

Creating the BlackBoardData

BlackBoardData functions as the memory unit of the brain of the NPC. This is where you store and retrieve data that would be used to control the behavior of the NPC. Go to **Content Browser,** and navigate to **Create | Miscellaneous | Blackboard**. Rename it `MyNPC_Brain`.

Adding a variable into BlackBoardData

Double-click on **MyNPC_Brain** to open the BlackBoardData editor. Click on **New Key**, select **Key Type** as **Vector**, and name it `TargetLocation`. This screenshot shows that **TargetLocation** is created correctly. Save and close the editor.

Creating a Behavior Tree

Behavior Tree is the logic path that NPC goes through to determine what course of action to take.

To create a Behavior Tree in Unreal Engine, go to **Content Browser** | **Create** | **Miscellaneous**, and then click on **Behavior Tree**. Rename it `MyNPC_BT`.

Double-click on **MyNPC_BT** to open the Behavior Tree editor. The following screenshot shows the setting that we want for **MyNPC_BT**. It should have **MyNPC_Brain** set as the BlackBoard asset. If it doesn't, search for **MyNPC_Brain** and assign it as the BlackBoard asset.

If you have already gone through the earlier exercise and are familiar with a Behavior Tree, you will notice that in this editor that there is a **Root** node, which you could use to start building out your NPC's behavior.

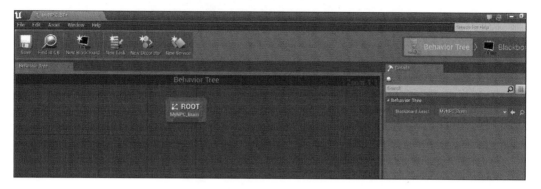

Creating a simple BT using a Wait task

The next step here is to add on a composite node (either **Sequence**, **Selector**, or **Simple Parallel**). In this example, we will select and use a **Sequence** node to extend our Behavior Tree here. You can click and drag from the **Root** node to open up the contextual menu, as shown in the following screenshot. Alternatively, just right-click to open up the menu and select the node that you want to create.

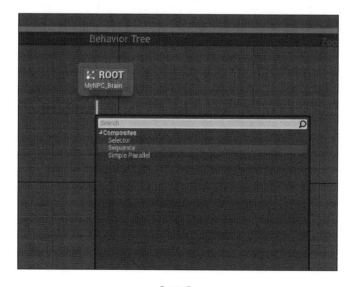

We will add a **Wait** task from the **Sequence** node. Click and drag to create a new connection from the **Sequence** node. From the contextual menu, select **Wait**. Set **Wait** to be **15.0s**, as shown in this screenshot. Save and compile **MyNPC_BT**.

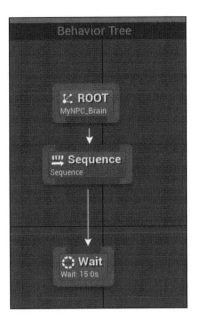

After compiling, click on **Play** in the Behavior Tree editor. You would see the light moving through the links and especially from the **Sequence** node to the **Wait** task for 15s.

Using the Behavior Tree

Now that we have a simple implementation of the Behavior Tree, we want our NPC character to start using it. How do we do this? Go to **Content Browser | MyFolder**, and double-click on **MyNPC_AIController** to open up the editor. Go to the **EventGraph** tab where we initially created a simple move forward implementation. Break the initial links between the **IsValid** node and **Add Movement Input**. Rewire them based on the following screenshot by linking the **IsValid** node to a new **Run** Behavior Tree node. In the **Run** Behavior Tree node, assign **BTAsset** to **MyNPC_BT**. Next, replace **Event Tick** with **Event Begin Play** (since the BT will now replace the thinking function here). Save and compile.

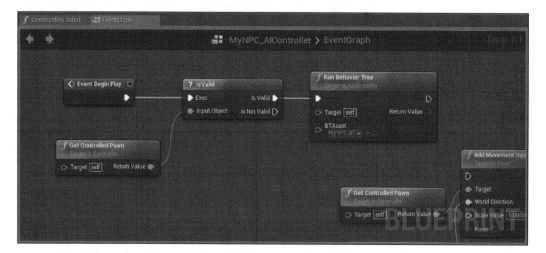

Creating a custom task for the Behavior Tree

We want to now make the NPC select a location on the map and walk toward it.

This requires the creation of a custom task where the NPC has to select a target location. We have already created an entry in the BlackBoardData to store a vector value. However, we have not made a way to assign values to the data yet. This would be done by creating a custom Behavior Tree task.

Go to **Content Browser | Create | Blueprint**. For the parent class, search for
BTNode and select **BTTask_BlueprintBase**, as shown in the following screenshot.
Rename this task as `Task_PickTargetLocation`.

Double-click on the newly created **Task_PickTargetLocation**. Go to **EventGraph**,
create the following nodes, and link these nodes:

- **Event Receive Execute**: Link **Owner Actor** to the target of **Get Actor
  Location**. When **PickTargetLocation** is executed, **Event Receive Execute**
  starts.

- **Get Actor Location**: Link **Return Value** to **Origin of Get Random Point** in
  the **Radius** node.

- **Set Blackboard Value as Vector**: Link **Event Receive Execute** to the
  execution arrow of **Set Blackboard Value as Vector**.

- **Get Random Point in Radius**: Link **Return Value** to the **Value** input for **Set
  Blackboard Value as Vector**.

- **Finish Execute**: Link **Set Blackboard Value as Vector** to the input execution of **Finish Execute**.

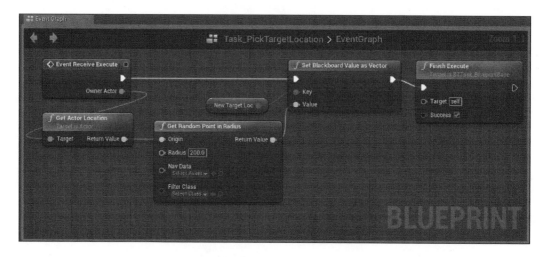

Notice that there is a **New Target Loc** variable linked to **Key** of **Set Blackboard Value as Vector**. We need to create a new variable for this. Click on **+Variable**, as shown in the following screenshot, to create a new variable. Name the new variable `New Target Loc`.

Click on the newly created **New Target Loc** to display the details of the variable. Select **BlackBoardKeySelector** as the variable type, as shown in this screenshot:

Save and compile the custom task.

Using the PickTargetLocation custom task in BT

Add a new link from the current **Sequence** composite node. Place the **Task_PickTargetLocation** node to the left of the **Sequence** node so that it would be executed first, as shown in the following screenshot. Make sure that **New Target Loc** is set as **TargetLocation**:

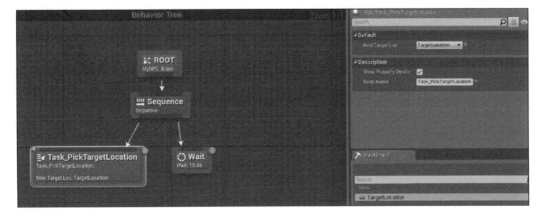

Replacing the Wait task with Move To

Delete the **Wait** node, and add the **Move To** node in its place. Make sure that **Blackboard Key** for **Move To** is set as **TargetLocation**, as show in this screenshot:

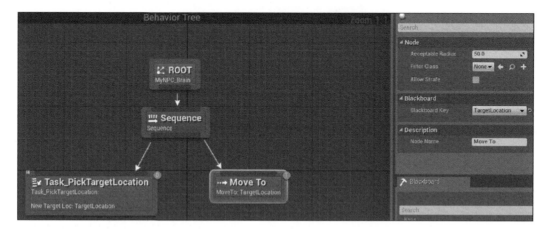

After compiling, click on **Play** to run the game. Double-click on **MyNPC_BT** to open the Behavior Tree editor. You would see the light moving through the links and the **TargetLocation** value changing in the Blackboard, as shown in this screenshot:

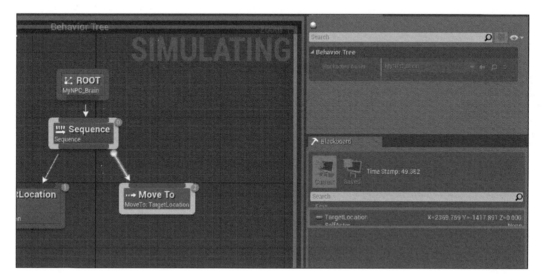

Remember to go back to the map level and see how the NPC is behaving now. The NPC now selects a target location and then move to the target location. Then, it selects a new target location and moves to another spot.

With this example, you have gained a detailed understanding of how to set up AI behavior and getting AI to work in your level. Challenge yourself to create more complex behaviors using the knowledge gained in this section.

Implementing AI in games

I am sure you have noticed that we definitely need to create more complex behaviors to make a game interesting. In terms of implementation, it is often easier to implement more complex AI through a combination of programming and use the editor functions to take this a step further. So, it is important to know how AI can be triggered via the editor and how you can customize AI for your game.

Summary

This chapter covers both animation and artificial intelligence. These are huge topics in game development and there is definitely more to learn about them. I hope that through this chapter, you now have a strong understanding of these two topics and will use your skills to further explore more functions in the Unreal Editor to create cooler stuff.

We learned a little about the history of animation, how animation is created today in 3D computer games through various 3D modeling software, and finally, how to import this animation into Unreal Engine to be used in games. An animation sequence is the format in which animation is stored/played in Unreal, and you've learned about a simple blend technique to combine different animation sequences.

Personally, I love how AI contributes to a game. In this chapter, you learned about the different components that make up AI logic. The main AI logic is executed through the Behavior Tree, and we learned how to construct a Behavior Tree in terms of logic as well as how to replicate this into the Unreal Editor itself through the use of BlackBoardData, Task, Composite, and other nodes.

Ending this chapter, we have covered a huge portion of what we need to create a game. In the next chapter, you will learn how to add sounds and particle effects into a game.

6
A Particle System and Sound

In this chapter, we will touch on the components of a game that are extremely important but often go unnoticed unless they are badly designed and out of place. Yes, we will cover particle system and sound in this chapter. In most games, they blend in so naturally that they are easily forgotten. They can also be used to create the most memorable moments in a game.

Just to recap, particle systems are used very often to create sparks, explosions, smoke, rain, snow, and other similar effects in a game that are dynamic, kind of fuzzy, and random in nature. Sound can be in the form of ambient sounds, such as the sound of rustling leaves and wind, one-off sounds, such as a pan dropping in the kitchen, or repetitive sounds, such as the running steps of a character or even music playing on the radio. Sound can be used to set the mood of a game, alert the player to something that needs attention, and provide realism to a level to make a place come alive. Let's get started.

What is a particle system?

A particle system is a way to model fuzzy objects, such as rain, fire, clouds, smoke, and water, which do not have smooth, well-defined surfaces and are nonrigid. The system is an optimized method to achieve such fluid-looking and dynamic visual representations by controlling the movement, behavior, interaction, and look of many tiny geometry objects or sprites.

Using a combination of different particles made of different shapes, sizes, materials, and textures, with different movement speeds, rotation direction/speeds, spawn rates, concentration, visibility duration, and many more factors, we are able to create a huge variety of dynamic complex systems.

In this chapter, we will learn about the components of the particle system using Unreal's Particle System editor and Cascade editor and use these editors to create a few additions for your level.

Exploring an existing particle system

We will start by first seeing what kind of particle systems we get in the default package of Unreal Engine 4. Go to **Content Browser | Game | Particles**. There are a couple of particle systems that we can already drag and place in the level and check out how they look.

To open a particle system, simply double-click on any of the systems. Let's take a look at **P_Fire** together. Feel free to check out the rest of the systems as well. However, I will use this as an example to understand what we need in order to create a new particle system for our level. This screenshot shows **P_Fire** in the editor:

On the left-hand side is **Viewport** where we can preview the particle system. On the right-hand side, in the **Emitters** tab, you can see several columns of boxes with **Flames** (twice), **Smoke**, **Embers**, and **Sparks** mentioned on top of each of the columns.

Emitters can be thought of as separate components that make up the particle system, and you can give each emitter different properties depending on what you want to create. When you put a bunch of emitters together, you will see them combining to give you a whole visual effect. In this **P_Fire** particle system, you can see flames moving in an unpredictable manner with some sparks and embers floating around and smoke simulating a fire bursting into flames. In the next section, let's go through more concrete terminology that describes the particle system in Unreal Engine 4.

The main components of a particle system

Very briefly, the following paragraph (taken from the official Unreal 4 documentation that's available online) very aptly describes the relationship between the different components that are used in particle systems:

> *"Modules, which define particle behavior and are placed within...Emitters, which are used to emit a specific type of particle for an effect, and any number of which can be placed within a...Particle System, which is an asset available in the Content Browser, and which can then in turn be referenced by an...Emitter Actor, which is a placeable object that exists within your level, controlling where and how the particles are used in your scene."*

Read this several times to make sure that you are clear on the relationship between the different components.

So, as described in the earlier section where we looked at **P_Fire**, we know that the emitters are labelled as **Flames**, **Embers**, **Sparks**, **Smoke**, and so on. The different properties of each of the emitters are defined by adding modules, such as **Lifetime**, **Initial Velocity**, and so on, into them. Together, all the emitters make up a particle system. Lastly, when you place the emitters in your game level, you are, in fact, dragging the emitter actor, which references a particular particle system.

Modules

The **Default Required** and **Spawn** modules are the modules that every emitter needs to have. There is also a long list of other optional modules that the Cascade Particle editor offers to customize your particle system. In the current version of the editor that I am using, I have the **Acceleration**, **Attractor**, **Beam**, **Camera**, **Collision**, **Color**, **Event**, **Kill**, **Lifetime**, **Location**, **Orbit**, **Orientation**, **Parameter**, **Rotation**, **Rotation Rate**, **Size**, **Spawn**, **SubUV**, **Vector Field**, and **Velocity** modules.

We will cover a few of the frequently used modules from this long list of modules through a simple exercise that's based on **P_Fire**. I understand that it would be very boring and not very useful when grasping the basics here if I simply gave you all those definitions that you can find easily online. Instead, we will go through this section by customizing **P_Fire** to create a fireplace for our level. At the same time, we will go through the key values within the different modules that you can adjust. Thus, you can take a look at how these values impact the look of the particle system.

For more detailed documentation on the definition of each module and parameter, you can refer to the Unreal 4 online documentation (`https://docs.unrealengine.com/latest/INT/Engine/Rendering/ParticleSystems/Reference/index.html`).

The commonly used modules are listed as follows:

Module	Key parameters it can control
Required	Material used for the particles
Spawn	Rate and distribution of the spawn
Initial Size	Size of the initial particle
Lifetime	Time duration for which the particle stays visible
Color Over Life	Color of the particles over their lifetimes

The design principles of a particle system

The design principles of a particle system can be configured through a research and iterative creative process. Let's take a look at each one of them in the following section.

Research

Details are probably key to designing a realistic particle system. Very often, creating a particle system lies in the realm of an artist as we need an artistic touch to create a visually appealing and somewhat realistic replica of the effect that we want to create.

For starters, it is good to research a little on what the actual effect looks like. Here are some steps to help you get started:

- Identify the different components that are needed (break the particle effects down into the different components).

- Determine the relationship among the different components (the size of the particles that are relative to one another, spawn rate, lifetimes, and so on).

- Next, look at other similar effects that are created in the **Computer Graphics (CG)** space. The reason for doing this is that sometimes, actual effects can be a little too monotonous, and there are many amazing visual effect people out there who you can learn from to spice things up a little. So, it is a great idea to spend a little time checking out what others have done already, rather than spending a whole lot of time experimenting and not getting what you want to achieve.

The iterative creative process

Creating the perfect looking particle system that you want usually involves quite a bit of tweaking and playing around with the parameters that you have. The key to doing this is knowing what parameters there are and what they affect. During the initial phase of design, you should also try adding or removing certain modules to see how they actually impact the overall look of the system. This does not mean that more is always better. Additionally, it is also wise to save backup copies of your iterations so that you can always go back to the previous versions easily.

Being extremely proficient in creating the particle system, I think, involves a combination of good design planning, having the patience to iterate, and making small adjustments to get the look that you eventually want.

Example – creating a fireplace particle system

In this example, we will duplicate **P_Fire** and edit it to create a fire for a fireplace in the level. We will also change a part of the current level in which we have to place this new fireplace particle system.

Go to **Content Browser** | **Particles**, select **P_Fire**, and duplicate it. Rename it P_ Fireplace. This screenshot shows how **P_Fireplace** is created in the Particles folder:

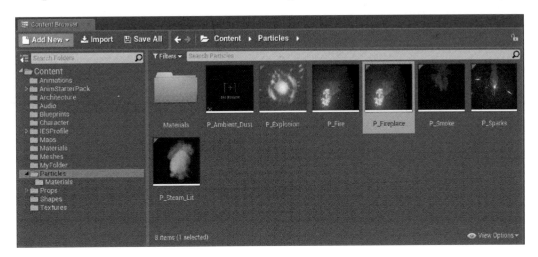

Let's open **Chapter5Level** and rename it `Chapter6Level` first. We will first add a fireplace structure to the level to set the context for this fireplace effect. This will help you follow the creation process better. This screenshot shows the original living room space:

The following screenshot shows the modified living room space with a fireplace:

This screenshot shows a zoomed in version of the fireplace structure if you intend to construct it:

Zooming in on the metal vents will look like this:

What we did here was delete the lights and low cabinet structure and replaced it with this:

- **TopWoodPanel** (material: **M_Wood_Walnut**): X = 120, Y = 550, Z = 60
- Concrete pillars around the glass (material: **M_Brick_Cut_Stone**)
- **ConcretePillar_L** and **ConcretePillar_R**: X = 100, Y = 150, Z = 220
- **ConcretePillar_Top**: X = 100, Y = 250, Z = 100
- Fireplace glass and inside (material: **M_Glass**)
- **Fireglass**: X = 5, Y = 250, Z = 120
- **MetalPanel** and **MetalPanel_Subtractive**: X = 40, Y = 160, Z = 10
- **FireVent1** to **FireVent5**

Use the BSP subtractive cylinder with the following setting, as shown in the following screenshot. Here, **Z** is **10**, **Outer Radius** is **3**, and **Sides** is **8**:

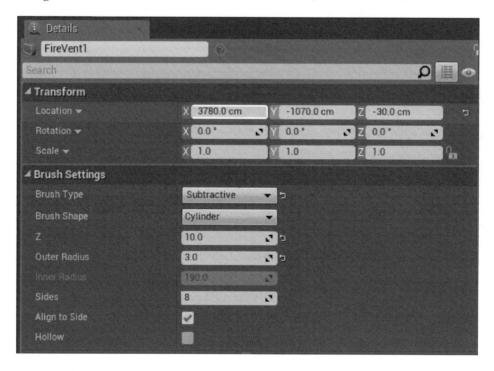

The lower extended structure (made up of two BSPs) consists of the following:

- **Thinner extension platform**: X = 140, Y = 550, Z = 10
- **Thicker base**: X = 120, Y = 550, Z = 30

Crafting P_Fireplace

Now, double-click on **P_Fireplace** to open up the Cascade Particle System editor. Since we duplicated it from **P_Fire**, it has the same emitters as **P_Fire**: the two **Flame**, one **Smoke**, one **Sparks**, one **Embers**, and one **Distortion** module.

Observe the current viewport. What do you see? The original **P_Fire** effect is more like a sequence of random bursts of flames that disappear pretty quickly after the initial burst. What kind of fire do we need for the fireplace that we have created? We need more or less continuous and slower moving flames that hover in a fixed position.

With this difference and objective in mind, we will next determine which of the components of **P_Fire** we want to keep as our fire effect for the fireplace.

Observing the solo emitters of the system

Using the solo button and checkbox in each of the modules, toggle **S** on or off, and alternatively mark/unmark the checkbox to observe the individual components. This screenshot shows you the location of the solo button and checkbox:

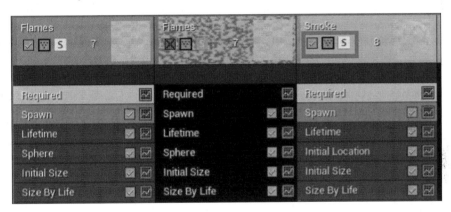

Deleting non-essential emitters

The first step was to delete the second **Flame** emitter (the first being the left-most) and the **Smoke** emitter. The reason for this was, I think, so that I could work with a single flame to create a fire for the fireplace. The **Smoke** emitter was removed mainly because of it is a gas/electric fire; thus, I would expect less smoke. You could alternatively unmark the checkbox at the top of the window to hide the entire emitter first before deleting it permanently.

Focusing on editing the Flame emitter

Keeping the only **Flame** emitter, the flame was still appearing at random spots within a certain radius and then disappearing quickly after that. We will address each of the issues here one by one:

- **Configure Lifetime**: So, since we need to have the fire burning continuously instead of in short bursts, I will first adjust the **Lifetime** property so that the fire burns for a longer period of time before disappearing. Change **Distribution Float Uniform**, with **Min** kept as **0.7**, **Max** as **1.0**, and **Distribution Constant** as **1.2**.

- **Remove Const Accleration+**: Now, the flame lingers longer on screen before disappearing. However, the flames seem to be drifting away from the spawn location after they are spawned. For a fireplace, flames more or less remain in the same location. So, I turn off **Const Acceleration+** in the **Flames** module by unmarking the checkbox. The flames now seem to be moving away from the spawn location a lot less.

- **Remove Initial Velocity**: After removing the acceleration module, it still seems like the flames are moving away; my guess for this is that the particles had some initial velocity, and so I turned off this module to confirm my suspicion and it seemed to work.

- **Configure Spawn**: The flames looked quite sparse as they are small, and this creates some blank space within the spawn area during short intervals. I could adjust the size of the flame to make it bigger, but when I did this, the flame looked too distorted. So, I decided to increase the spawn rate instead so that more flames could occur per minute. Change the spawn rate for **Rate Scale Distribution** from **5.0** to **20.0**. Increase **Distribution Float Constant** from **1.0** to **3.0**.

Looking at the complete particle system

Now, I've turned the other emitters back on again to look at the whole particle system effect and also see if it requires more editing. It looks pretty okay for a fireplace fire now so I've stopped here. Feel free to go ahead and adjust the other properties to improve the design. These are the very basics of modifying an existing particle system, and I hope you have familiarized yourself with the particle system editor through this exercise.

Sound and music

Sound and music are an essential part of the game experience. Ever watched television with the volume switched off? Just watching subtitles and lip movements is not enough. You want to hear what the character on the screen is saying and how they are saying it. For games, it is pretty much similar, and on top of this, pretty often, you get cues through the sound and music. If you have played *Alien: Isolation*, you need to listen to the sounds in the game to know whether you have an alien coming in your direction. This can be a matter of life and death in the game. It pretty much determines whether you end up as a winner or simply a delicious meal for the alien. So, are we ready now to learn how sound and music are created for games, and how we use the Unreal Editor to incorporate them into our game level?

How do we produce sound and music for games?

Many game productions have original music written for in-game scenarios; some also use actual songs sung by professional singers as theme songs. Music in games is a big thing and it's dearly remembered by fans of the game. Sometimes, the music itself is enough to trigger memories of the gaming experience. Thus, game studios need to spend time creating suitable music to complement their games.

If you are a huge fan of video game music, there are also concerts that you can go to where the orchestra plays music from popular games (check out Video Games Live at http://www.videogameslive.com/index.php?s=home).

Creating music for a game is very similar to composing music for a piece; it should trigger appropriate emotions when it's played. The choice of music needs to match the pace and situations of the game. Using a JRPG game as an example, you should be able to differentiate between in-battle music versus the music that's played when you are in a menu, loading the game, or when you've just won a battle. Very often, music is created on the basis of the needs of the game, and the music composer has to probably come up with a few different versions and let the team and/or management review it before the best piece is selected.

If you do not intend to create original music or sound for your game, you can find many free downloadable sounds and music online these days. When using free online music and sounds, do ensure that you do not violate any digital rights or copyrights when incorporating them in your game.

Audio quality

The reason why we are discussing audio quality is because sound quality, like image quality, is of huge importance these days. We already use the 4K resolution image quality today, and there will be more devices and games that would support this in the future. How about sounds? The listening experience needs to match the quality of the image and provide more than just mono or stereo sounds. Sound experience has also progressed to multichannel surround sound, starting at 5.1, 7.1, and beyond these days, to obtain a life-like immersive audio experience. This is definitely something to think about when creating, storing, and playing audio files.

How are sounds recorded?

Sounds are generated in the form of analog waves, which are continuous waves, which you'll see shortly in the upcoming figure. We can record surround sound through a recording device. For multichannel sound recording, you need to have certain methods to record music that can use a simple recording setup known as **Deca Tree**. Here, microphones are placed in a particular fashion to capture sounds from the left, right, front, and back of the source. There are also many processing techniques that can filter and convert sounds that are recorded to mimic the various components needed for each of the channels.

We take samples of the analog sound waves that are produced by a piano at close intervals (the rate at which the samples are taken between intervals is known as sampling frequency). The process of taking samples from analog waves to store them digitally is known as **Pulse Code Modulation (PCM)**. These samples can be stored in uncompressed PCM-like formats or be compressed into a smaller and more manageable file size using audio compression techniques. Wav, MP3, Ogg Vorbis, Dolby TrueHD, and DTS-HD are some of the formats that audio is commonly saved as. Ideally, we want to save audio into a lossless compressed format so that we get a small manageable file that contains amazing sounds.

When the digital format of the sound is played back, the analog sound wave is reconstructed using the stored information. Close resemblance to the original analog sound waves is one way to ensure sounds of good quality. By increasing the number of channels to create a 3D sound effect using the basic 5.1 surround, which requires five speakers, one for front left, one front right, one center, one back left (as surround), one back right (as surround) and a subwoofer, also greatly improves the listening experience.

The Unreal audio system

We now have a general understanding of why we need audio in games and how it's created and recorded. Let's learn about the Unreal audio system and the editor that can be used to import these audio files into the game, and we'll also learn about the tools that can be used to edit and control playbacks.

Getting audio into Unreal

How do we get the audio files into Unreal? What do you need to take note of?

The audio format

Unreal supports the importing of sounds only in the `.wav` format. The `.wav` format is a widely used format that can store raw uncompressed sound data.

The sampling rate

The sampling rate is recommended at 44100 Hz or 22050 Hz. As mentioned earlier, the sampling rate determines how often the analog wave is recorded. The higher the frequency (measured in Hertz or Hz), the more data points of the analog wave that are collected, which aids in a better reconstruction of the wave.

Bit depth

The bit depth is set as 16. It determines the granularity at which the amplitude of the audio wave can be recorded, which is also known as the resolution of the sound. For a bit depth of 16, you can get up to 65,536 integer values (2^{16}). The reason why we are concerned with the bit depth is because during the sampling process of the analog waves, the actual value of the amplitude of the wave is approximated to one of the integer values that can be stored based on the bit depth. The following figure shows two different bit depths. The figure on the left-hand side illustrates when the bit depth is low, and the signal is more inaccurately sampled because it is sampled in larger increments. The figure on the right-hand side illustrates when the bit depth is higher, and it can be sampled at smaller increments, resulting in a more accurate representation of the wave:

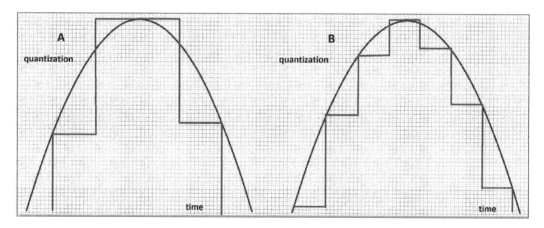

The loss in accuracy of the representation of the wave can be termed as a quantization error. When the bit depth is too low, the quantization error is high.

The **Signal to Quantization Noise Ratio (SQNR)** is the measurement used to determine the quality of this conversion. It is calculated using the ratio between the maximum nominal signal strength and the quantization error. The better the ratio, the better the conversion.

Supported sound channels

Unreal currently supports channels such as mono, stereo, 2.1, 4.1, 5.1 6.1, and 7.1.

When importing files into Unreal, take note of the file naming convention that is in place so that the right sound is played from the right channel.

The following table shows the 7.1 surround sound configuration with all the file naming conventions that are necessary for the correct playback:

Speakers	Front-left		Front-center		Front-right
Extension	_fl		_fc		_fr
Speakers	Side-left		Low frequency (commonly known as subwoofer)		Side-right
Extension	_sl		_lf		_sr
Speakers	Back-left				Back-right
Extension	_bl				_br

This table shows you the files that are used for the 5.1 surround system:

Speakers	Front-left		Front-center		Front-right
Extension	_fl		_fc		_fr
Speakers	Side-left		Low frequency (commonly known as subwoofer)		Side-right
Extension	_sl		_lf		_sr

This table shows you the files that are used for the 4.0 system:

Speakers	Front-left				Front-right
Extension	_fl				_fr
Speakers	Side-left				Side-right
Extension	_sl				_sr

Unreal sound formats and terminologies

There are a couple of terms in the Unreal Sound system that we need to get acquainted with:

- **Sound waves**: These are the actual audio files that are in the .wav format.

- **Sound cues**: This is the control system for a sound wave file. Sound cues are what we use to manipulate the volume, start, and end of the sound waves. So, in order to control how an audio file is played in the game, you can edit the properties on the Sound Cue, which, in turn, affects the wave file or files that it is associated with.

- **Ambient Sound Actor**: This is the class actor that you add to the game level. This actor is associated with the Sound Cue to play the audio files that you need for the game.

Now, we are ready to use the Sound Editor in Unreal.

The Sound Cue Editor

Since we are not editing the actual audio file per se, the sound editor in Unreal is known as the Sound Cue Editor. We are, in fact, editing the way the sound can be played through a control device known as a Sound Cue.

Let's learn more about the functionalities of the Sound Cue Editor.

How to open the Sound Cue Editor

Go to **Content Browser** | **Audio**. Go to any Sound Cue file, and double-click to open the Sound Cue Editor. This screenshot shows where I could find a Sound Cue in **Content Browser**:

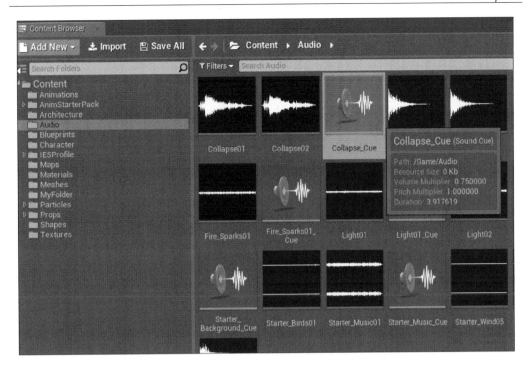

When you double-click on a Sound Cue, the Sound Cue Editor opens up, and it looks quite a lot like the Blueprint Editor with modules and lines. This screenshot shows you what the Sound Cue Editor for **Collapse_Cue** looks like:

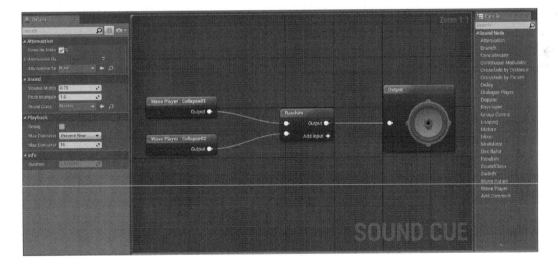

Notice that in the preceding screenshot **Collapse_Cue** it has two inputs called **Wave Player: Collapse 01** and **Wave Player: Collapse 02**. These are joined to a **Random** node, and the output goes to the final node known as **Output**. What this does is that when this Sound Cue is played, one of the two collapse sounds gets randomly selected and is played. This creates a variety when sounds are played in the same circumstance; they are both collapse sound effects but slightly different.

We will learn more about the components that we could use to design the Sound Cues later. We'll also go through an exercise later to create our own Sound Cue in the editor.

Exercise – importing a sound into the Unreal Editor

You may come across a situation where you have created your own audio effect file and want to use it in the game. We will first start by importing this file.

For this exercise, I have used an audio clip downloaded from a Wikipedia site (`https://en.wikipedia.org/wiki/The_Four_Seasons_(Vivaldi)`) with a Vivaldi piece from The Four Seasons. This is shared by John Harrison.

This file is in the Oggs format, and yes, Unreal only supports `.wav` files. First, I converted the file type from `.ogg` to `.wav` using software that's listed on the Vorbis website at `http://vorbis.com/software/`. Be careful about the WAV file settings that Unreal is expecting it to be in.

After getting the right wav file, we are ready to import it into the Sound Editor. Go to **Content Browser | Content | Audio**, right-click on it to display the contextual menu, navigate to **New Asset | Import to /Game/Audio**, and browse to the folder where you saved the `.wav` file and select it. This screenshot shows where you can find the function in the editor to import the `.wav` file:

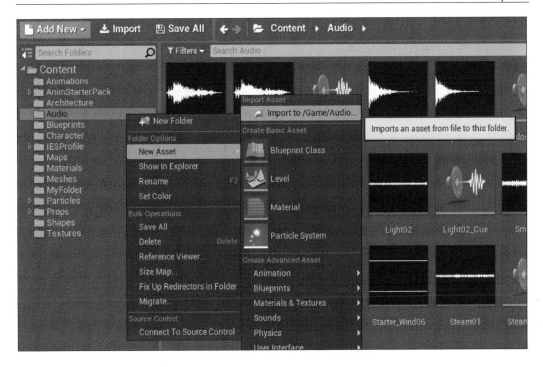

This screenshot shows you how the Vivaldi WAV file is successfully imported as a sound wave in the Audio folder with the WAV file settings:

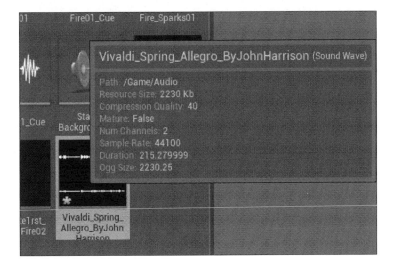

Next, create a Sound Cue for the Vivaldi sound wave that we have just imported. To recap, a Sound Cue is used to control the playback of the sound wave file. A sound wave file merely has the contents of the audio file. Right-click on the sound wave asset, as shown in this screenshot, and select **Create Cue** in the contextual menu:

Double-click on the newly created Sound Cue (which has a default name with the same name as the sound wave file with a `Cue` suffix). In the example here, it will be `Vivaldi_Spring_Allegro_ByJohnHarrison_Cue`. Double-click on this Cue to view the contents. The following screenshot shows the contents of `Vivaldi_Spring_Allegro_ByJohnHarrison_Cue`. The wave player output is connected directly to **Output**. This is the simplest connection for a Sound Cue where we input the wave to the **Output**.

Now, let's hear the sound we have imported. Within the Sound Cue Editor, look for the **Play Cue** button in the top-left corner of the editor. Take a look at the following screenshot for location of the button. After clicking the button, you would hear the music we have just imported. You have just successfully imported a custom wave file into Unreal. Now, let's transfer it to the game level.

Exercise – adding custom sounds to a level

In order to place sound in the level, you need to use the **Ambient Sound** node to associate it with a sound cue, which would, in turn, play the audio files.

To create an **Ambient Sound** node, go to **Modes | All Classes,** drag and drop **Ambient Sound** into the game level:

Click on the Ambient Sound Actor that you have just placed into the level, and rename it AmbientSound_Vivaldi. In the **Details** panel, scroll to the **Sound** section, click on the arrow next to **Sound** to display the sound assets that you have in the game level packages, as shown in the following screenshot. Select **Vivaldi_Spring_Allegro_ByJohnHarrison_Cue**.

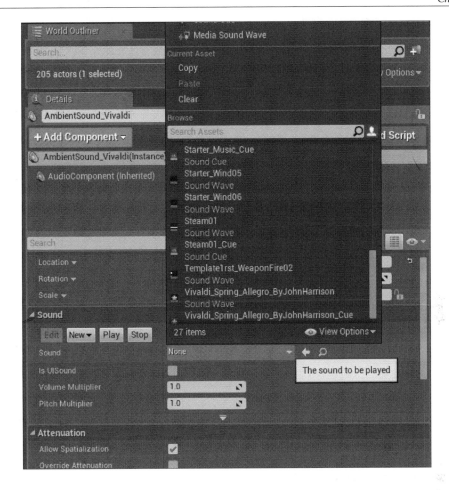

Check whether you can still hear the music by clicking on the **Play** button in the **Details** panel of **AmbientSound_Vivaldi**. Now, let's build the level and run it. Notice that the music plays when you start the level.

Configuring the Sound Cue Editor

Double-click on **Vivaldi_Spring_Allegro_ByJohnHarrison_Cue** to open the Sound Cue Editor. Notice that on the right-hand side, there is **Palette** with a list of nodes, as shown in the following screenshot. These nodes can be used to control how the sounds are played or heard.

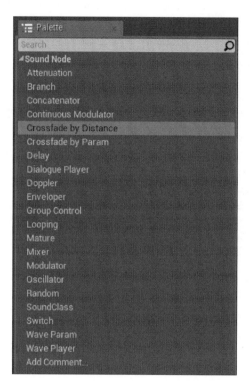

If you find that your sound design cannot be achieved using the nodes in the list, you can alternatively request for new nodes to be created via the UE4 source code.

Summary

Both particles and sound are very interesting components of a game and require very specialized skills that are very apt for their design and creation. Particle system creators often have strong artistic and technical backgrounds; an artistic touch is needed to create suitable textures, and a technical ability helps to adjust distributions/values that create an appropriate overall effect. Audio engineers often have a strong music background. They are probably composers and musicians themselves with a passion for games.

In the first half of the chapter, we learned about what a particle system is. We learned how particle systems are used to create in-game effects, such as falling snow, rainfall, flames, fireworks, explosion effects, and much more. A particle system can efficiently render small moving fuzzy particles using textures through a combination of emitters. Each emitter has many configurable modules that can control properties, such as a spawn rate, lifetime, velocity, and the acceleration needed to create the required effect. In this chapter, we covered how to edit an existing fire explosion particle system, turn it into a fireplace effect, and place it in a living room. Through this example, we also went through some basic principles that could be applied to the particle system design process, and how to make minor adjustments to a few popular basic modules to create the effect we wanted.

The second half of the chapter covered how to include sounds in a level. We learned how sounds/music are conceptualized, created, recorded, and eventually, imported into the Unreal Editor. We also covered the audio format that the Unreal Editor currently supports, and a little explanation of each of the components is given to give you a better insight into sounds. Next, we went through a simple exercise to import an online audio file and get the music we have downloaded playing in the game level.

I hope you have gained a little more understanding about the creation process of the particle system and the audio effects that are needed for the games in this chapter. We will continue to improve our game level with a little terrain editing and also create cinematic effects in the next chapter.

7
Terrain and Cinematics

In this chapter, we will cover a few level-enhancing features. We will create some outdoor terrain for our level as well as add a short cinematic sequence at the start of the game level.

In this chapter, we will look at the following topics:

- Creating an outdoor terrain
- Adding a shortcut for a cinematic sequence at the beginning of the same level

Introducing terrain manipulation

Terrain manipulation is needed when you want to create large natural landscape areas, such as mountainous or valley areas that are covered with foliage. This can be in the form of trees/grass, lakes, and rivers that are covered with rocks or snow, and so on. The Landscape tool in Unreal Engine 4 allows you to creatively design a variety of terrains for your game maps easily, while allowing the game to run at a reasonable frame rate.

When playing in a map that has large outdoor terrains, for example, maps with a large number of trees or many elevations, such as mountains, the effective frame rate is expected to be reduced due to an increase in the number of polygons that need to be rendered on the screen. Hence, being well-versed in landscaping so that polygon counts are kept under control is important to ensure that the map is actually playable. It is also good to bear in mind to make use of optimization techniques, such as LOD and fog to mask the distant places, which can give you a sense of unending open land.

- If you are planning to create an open world, you can also use the Procedural Foliage tool (available in Unreal 4.8 and higher versions) to spawn these features for you.

Let's get ourselves familiarized with the Unreal Landscaping tool and start creating some outdoor environments for our game level. We will learn how to perform simple contouring of the outdoor space with low hills, grass, and trees. Then, we will create a small pond in the area. For more accurate landscaping, we can import a height map to help us with the creation of the landscape.

Exercise – creating hills using the Landscape tool

Let's perform the following steps to create hills using the Landscape tool:

1. Open `Chapter6.umap` and save it under `Chapter7_Terrain.umap`.

2. Go to **Modes**, click on the Landscape tool (the icon looks like a mountain) and then click on **Manage**.

3. Select **Create New** (the other option here is to make use of a height map, which we will cover later in the chapter).

4. To select a Material, you can click on the search icon and type `M_Ground_Grass`, or go to **Content Browser | Content | Materials**, select **M_Ground_Grass**, and click on the arrow next to **Landscape Material** to assign the material.

5. For this example, we are going to leave all of the landscape settings at their default values that are listed, as follows. The next section will explain the options for the rest of the values in further detail:

   ° **Scale**: X = 100 Y = 100 Z = 100

   ° **Section Size**: 63 x 63 quads

   ° **Section Per Component**: 1 x 1 section

   ° **Number of Components**: 8 x 8

   ° **Overall Resolution**: 505 x 505

The following screenshot shows the top view of the grass landscape that we have created. Notice the 64 green squares. You will need to switch to the **Top** view to view it.

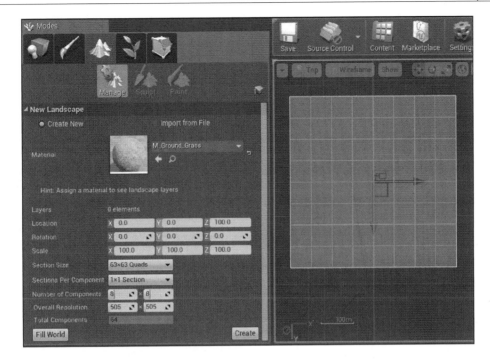

Now, we'll switch over to the **Perspective** view. The grass landscape seems like it's covering half the house. Take a look at the following screenshot:

Note that if we had created the landscape on an empty map, we would not have this issue, as we would have built the house on the landscape grass instead. So, we have to perform an additional step here to move the landscape grass under the house so that we do not have a house that's submerged under the grass. You need to select **Landscape** and **LandscapeGizmoActiveActor** from **World Outliner**, as shown on the right-hand side of the following screenshot. Remember to switch **Mode** back to **Place**, instead of the **Landscape** we were in to create the grass. The **Place** mode allows the translation/rotation of the selected object. Move the grass to just below the house, as shown in the following screenshot:

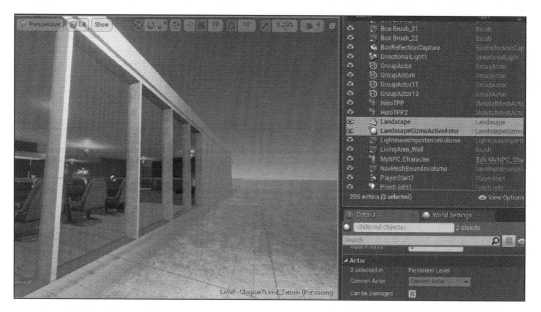

 Note that this step is performed because we add the landscape grass after we've built the house.

Now, we are ready to sculpt this flat land into some terrain. Go to **Modes** | **Landscape** | **Sculpt** again. Use the Sculpt tool, **Circle Brush**, and the **Smooth Falloff** combination, as shown in the upcoming screenshot. The default settings should be as follows:

- **Brush Size: 2048**
- **Brush Falloff: 0.5**
- **Tool Strength: 0.3**

To illustrate the size of the 2048 brush, I have switched to the **Top** view:

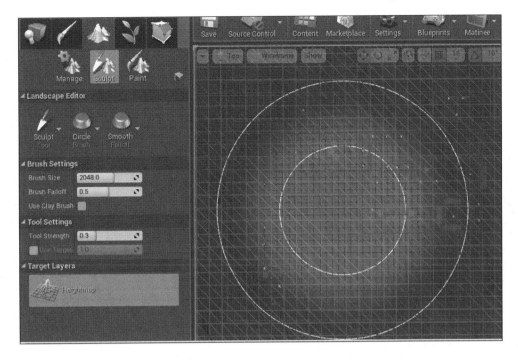

When **Brush Size** is set to **1000**, the brush radius is reduced, as shown in the following screenshot:

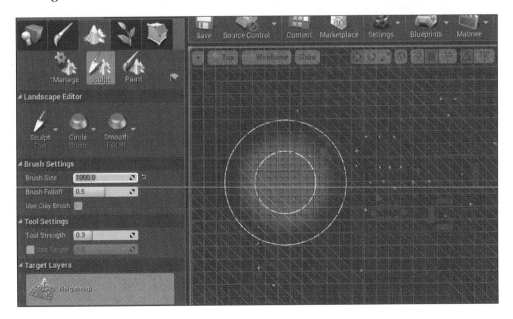

Now that we have an idea about the difference in radii, we will switch back to the **Perspective** view. Position your working screen to a slightly angled top perspective view, as shown in the following screenshot. Set **Brush size** to **1000** and **Tool Strength** to **0.4**:

Start by creating low hills around the house by clicking on the area around the house. I used a mix between a brush size of 1000 and 2048.

The following screenshot shows how the area looked after I worked on it for a bit. Note that the area in front of the wide windows where I created a depression. This is achieved by holding *Ctrl* and then clicking on the area. This depression will take the form of a lake in front of the dining area.

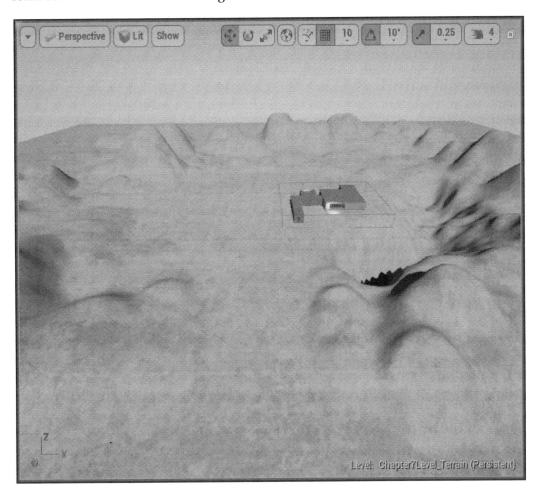

Create two box BSPs to fill up the depressed area. Apply the Lake Water material to the box BSPs. The following screenshot shows the same area with the box BSPs put in place. Use the Translation tool to keep both BSP areas on the same ground level at the location of the depression.

Next, I touched up the external area of the house. Use the **Unlit** mode to help you see the house better. This screenshot shows you how the house and area around it look after touching them up with the **MyGreyWall** material:

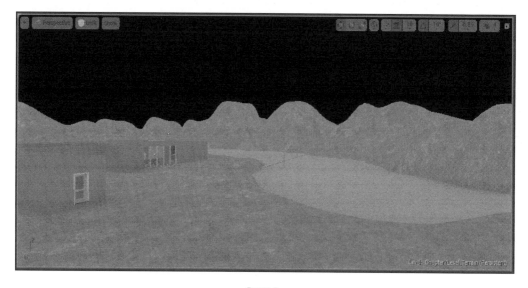

Go back to the **Lit** mode, build the level, and then take a look at it. Adjust any lighting in the map so that it's lit up appropriately. Rebuild until you are satisfied with what you get.

Add trees and plants to make the area a little more realistic. I have downloaded a package from Marketplace that has some foliage to help me with this.

Go to Marketplace on the Unreal Start Page. Under **Environments**, look for free downloadable content called **Open World Demo Collection**. The following screenshot shows free **Open World Demo Collection** in Marketplace. After downloading the package, add it to the project that you are working on.

We now have a basic outdoor terrain for our map.

Landscape creation options

After going through the preceding exercise, you now have a good idea about how landscaping in Unreal Engine 4 fundamentally functions. In this section, we will add to the skills we have acquired so far and learn how to adjust or utilize features/functions of the Landscaping tool that is available to us.

Multiple landscapes

It is possible to have multiple landscapes in the same map. This allows you to split the creation process into different layers. If you have more than one landscape in the map, you will need to select a layer before modifying it.

Using custom material

You can import any material you want to use for the landscape; you can make your own grass, crops, sand texture, and so on. Since the custom material is mostly used for large areas of the map, it is good to bear in mind that you need to keep the material repeatable and optimized.

Importing height maps and layers

Why do we use height maps in landscaping? These allow a quicker and more precise way to create elevations/troughs in the Unreal Editor. For example, we can use a height map to store elevation information for a mountain that is 3000m in height and of a certain diameter. When we import the height map, the terrain is automatically shaped according to it. It is definitely a time-saving method that helps us create more precise landscape features without having to click, click, click to sculpt.

Height maps and layers can first be created externally using common tools, such as Photoshop, World Machine, ZBrush, and Mudbox by artists. Detailed instructions need to be followed to ensure the successful importation of the height map. This can be found in the Unreal Engine 4 documentation at `https://docs.unrealengine.com/latest/INT/Engine/Landscape/Custom/index.html`.

Scale

The **Scale** settings determine the scaling of the landscape. We have used X: 100 and Y: 100 to give us the area of the land that this landscape will cover. The Z value is kept as 100 to provide some height to create elevation.

The number of components

A component is the basic unit for rendering and culling. There is a fixed cost that's associated with the overall number of components; hence, it is capped at 32 x 32. Going beyond this value would affect the performance of your game level.

Section Size

Section Size determines how large each section is. It determines how the landscape is divided up. Large sections mean fewer overall components because the pie is divided into larger chunks. Fewer chunks to manage indicate a lower overall CPU cost.

However, a large section is not as effective when managing the LOD as compared to a smaller section. When there are smaller sections, we also get smaller component sizes (when the pie is of the same size, cutting it into smaller chunks indicates that you have less on your plate if you take one chunk). Since components are the basic unit used for culling and rendering, this means quicker responses to LOD changes due to the reduced area. LOD determines the number of vertices that need to be calculated. If LOD is more effective, we have fewer calculations to do, and the CPU cost is more optimized with smaller sections.

The catch here is balancing the size of the sections to avoid having too many components to go through and too few components might result in poor LOD management.

Sections Per Component

You have options ranging from 1 x 1 or 2 x 2 sections per component. What this means is that you have the option of having either one or four sections in each component. Since a component is the most basic unit in rendering and culling, for the 1 x 1 section, you can have one section rendered at the same time. For 2 x 2 sections per component, you can have four sections rendered at the same time. To limit the number of calculations needed to render a component, the size of each section should not be too large.

Introducing cinematics

Cinematics were developed largely for motion pictures, films, and movies. Today, we apply cinematic techniques to non-interactive game sequences, known as **cut scenes**, to enhance the gaming experience. The overall gaming experience has to be designed with cut scenes in mind as they usually fulfil certain game design objectives. These objectives are often slotted in between gameplay to enrich the storytelling experience in games.

Very much like shooting a movie, we would need to decide what kind of shots need to be taken, which angles to shoot from, how much zooming is needed, how many cameras to use, and what path the camera needs to take in order to develop a motion picture sequence of our object/objects of focus. The techniques employed to create this clip are known as **cinematic techniques**.

So, in this chapter, we will first go through a few key objectives that explain why cinematics are needed in games, and you learn a couple of simple cinematic techniques that we could use. You will also learn about the tools that Unreal Engine 4 offers to apply the techniques we have learned in order to create appropriate cinematic sequences for your game.

Cinematic techniques are created by cinematic experts who focus on creating cut scenes for your games. Alternatively, you could also engage a cinematic creation contracting company to get this done for you professionally.

Why do we need cut scenes?

When a game is designed, a fair amount of the game designing time is put into designing how players interact with the objects in the game and how this interaction can be made fun. The interactive portion of the game needs to be supplemented and cut scenes can help fill the gaps.

Cut scenes can be employed in games to help designers tell a story when you are playing the game. This technique can be employed before the game begins to draw the players into the mission itself and justifies why a mission has to be accomplished for the player. This helps the player to understand the storyline, create meaning for their actions, and draw the player into the game.

Another objective of cut scenes can be to highlight key areas in the game in order to give the players a glimpse of what to expect and provide subtle hints to successfully win the game. This information would be useful, especially in difficult to beat game levels or when the player is meeting the chief monster in the game.

Game designers also sometimes use cut scenes to reward players after a difficult battle. They amplify the effect of their success and play out the happy ending of their win in order to create positive emotions in the players. I am sure that there are endless creative ways to utilize cut scenes in games and how we could positively include them to enhance the gaming experience.

However, it is necessary to ensure that the use of cut scenes is justified well because cut scenes actually take the control of the game away from the player. Games are expected to be interactive, and we do not want to convert this into a passive multimedia experience when there are too many cut scenes.

Keeping these basic game design objectives in mind, let's now explore some technical cinematic fundamentals that will provide you the groundwork to design your own cinematics in games.

Cinematic techniques

The camera is the main tool that's used to create effects for cinematics. You can achieve various cinematic effects by adjusting the camera functions and finding/moving the camera to a good spot to capture a significant key object(s) of interest. This section will provide some technical terms that you can use to describe to your coworker/contractor how a particular cinematic sequence should be recorded.

Adjusted camera functions

Here are some commonly used functions that you can adjust on a camera to capture a scene.

Zoom

Zooming in on an object gives you a closer view on the object; providing more details about it. Zooming out takes your view further away from the object; it provides a perspective for the object with regard to its surroundings.

Zooming is achieved by adjusting the focal length of the camera lens; the camera itself stays in the same position.

Field of view

Field of view (FOV) is the area that is visible from a particular position and orientation in space. FOV for a camera is dependent on the lens and can be expressed as $FOV = 2\ arctan(SensorSize/2f)$, where f is the focal length.

For humans, FOV is the area that we can see without moving our head. The horizontal FOV kind of ends at the outer corner of the eye, as shown in the following image, which is about 62 degrees to the left-hand side and right-hand side (source: `http://buildmedia.com/what-are-survey-accurate-visual-simulations/`):

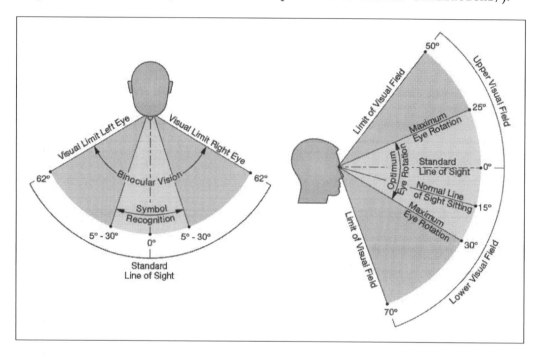

What this means is that whatever is outside this FOV is not visible to the entity.

Depth of field

Depth of field (DOF) is best expressed as a photo, such as the following one, where only the object of interest is very sharp and anything behind is it blurred. In the following image (source: `http://vegnews.com/articles/page.do?catId=2&pageId=2125`), the gyoza/dumplings appear sharp and beyond these, the bowl/bottle is blurred. The small DOF in the photo allows the foreground (gyoza) to be emphasized and the background to be de-emphasized. This is a very good technique to bring visual attention to objects of interest in photography as well as in cinematics.

DOF is also known to provide an effective focus range. The method to determine this range is to measure the distance between the closest object and farthest object in a scene that appears to be sharp in an image. Although a lens is made to focus on one distance at a time, the gradual decrease in sharpness is difficult to perceive under normal viewing conditions.

Camera movement

In filming, the camera is positioned at different angles and locations, and the camera moves with the actor/vehicle and so on. This camera movement can be described using some of the terms here.

Tilt

The camera is moved in a similar way to how you nod your head. The camera is pivoted at a fixed spot, and turning it up/down is known as tilting. The following figure shows the side view of the camera with arrows illustrating the tilting:

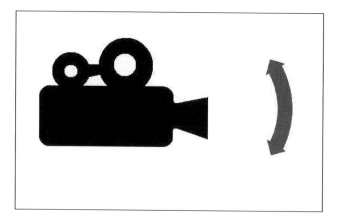

Pan

The camera is moved in a similar way to how you turn your head to look to the left-hand side and the right-hand side. The camera is pivoted at a fixed spot and turning it to the left-hand side/right-hand side is known as **panning**. This figure shows the top view of the camera with arrows demonstrating how panning works:

Dolly/track/truck

A dolly moves the entire camera toward or away from the object. It is quite similar to zooming in/out since you also going closer/further to the object, except that dollying moves the camera along a path toward/away from the object.

Trucking moves the camera sideways, that is, to the left-hand side or right-hand, along a track. Trucking is often confused with panning. The entire camera moves in trucking, but in panning, the camera stays in a fixed location and only the lens is swept to the left-hand side/right-hand side. Tracking is a specific form of trucking as it follows an object of interest in parallel. The following figure shows the back view of a camera dollying along a path:

Pedestal

Pedestal is the moving of the camera up and down a vertical track. The following figure illustrates the camera moving up and down a vertical track:

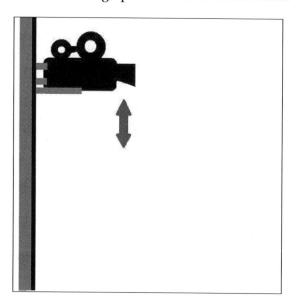

Capturing a scene

When capturing a scene, the overall scene is what matters most. You need to keep certain things in mind, such as what comprises the scene and its lighting; what you select determines how impactful the cut scene is. Here are a few factors that need to be addressed when composing a good cut scene.

Lighting

Light affects how a scene shows up in photo/cut scene. We need to have the right lighting in place to capture the mood of the scene.

Framing

Framing decides how the shot needs to be taken. Everything in the frame is important and you should pay attention to everything that is within the frame. How each shot transitions to the next also needs to be considered when creating a cut scene.

Some framing rules

The framing rules are as follows:

- Make sure the horizontals are level in the frame and the verticals are straight up along the frame.
- The Rule of Thirds. This rule divides the frame into nine sections. The points of interest should occur at one-third or two-thirds of the way up (or across) the frame rather than in the center. For example, the sky takes up approx. Two-thirds of this frame.
- Strategic empty spaces are provided in front, above, or behind the subject to allow space for the subject to move into/look into.
- Avoid having half an object captured in the frame.

Shot types

Here are some terms used to describe shots that can be taken for the frame:

- **Extreme Wide Shot (EWS) / Extreme Long Shot (ELS)**: This shot puts the subject into the environment. The shot is taken from a distance so that the environment around the subject can be seen. This type of a shot is very often used to establish a scene.
- **Wide Shot (WS) / Long Shot (LS)**: In a wide or long shot, the subject takes up the full frame. The subject is in the frame entirely with little space around it.
- **Medium Shot (MS)**: The medium shot has more of the subject in the frame and less of the environment.
- **Close Up Shot (CU)**: The subject covers approximately half the frame. This increases the focus on the subject.
- **Extreme Close Up Shot (ECU)**: The camera focuses on an important part of the subject.

Shot plan

This is a plan that describes how the scene will be captured. It also describes how many cameras to use, the sequence in which the cameras come on, and the kind of shots that need to be taken in order to play out the required effect for the scene.

Getting familiar with the Unreal Matinee Editor

The Unreal Matinee Editor is similar to nonlinear video editors, so it is quite easy to pick up if you already have experience using software such as Adobe Flash. Creating keyframes for cameras and moving them along paths combined with modifying camera properties creates the matinee/cut scene for games. Additionally, you can also make or convert static objects to become dynamic and then animate them using this Matinee Editor.

Exercise – creating a simple matinee sequence

Now, let's get hands-on and create a simple matinee sequence for your game. The plan is to showcase the area that we created at the beginning of the game. We will start with an extreme wide shot taken from the front of the house. We will use the dolly to take the camera toward the large windows in the dining area, into the kitchen area, and then the fireplace. Then, using the second camera, from the corner of the room, we will move toward a running guy and focus on his face.

Create a new matinee sequence from the ribbon, as shown in the following screenshot. Click on **Matinee** and select **Add Matinee**:

This opens up the Matinee Editor, as shown in the following screenshot:

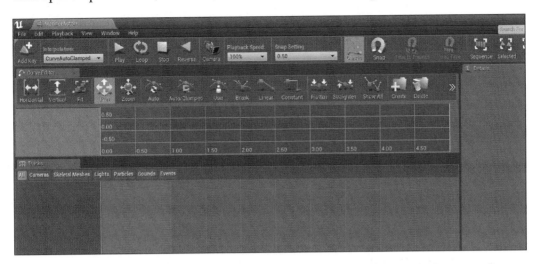

To create the first camera, we will right-click on the **Tracks** area and select **Add New Camera Group**:

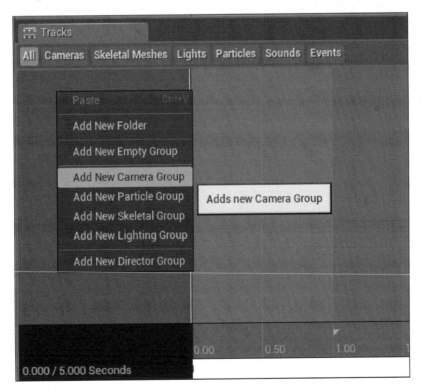

Going back to the map, you can see a small window in the corner of the map that shows what the camera is looking at. This screenshot shows where our first shot starts:

To create the next key where the next shot has to be taken, go back to the **Camera1** track, click on the small red arrow at 0.0 in the **Movement** row, and hit *Enter*. This duplicates the key. Press *Ctrl* and click and drag the red arrow to 2.00. This screenshot shows how to do it correctly:

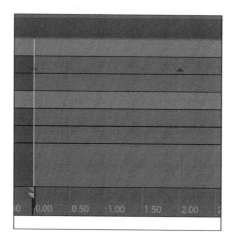

Now, click on the red arrow at 2.00 and go back to **Camera1** in the map. Right-click on it and select **Pilot 'Camera Actor1'**, as shown in this screenshot:

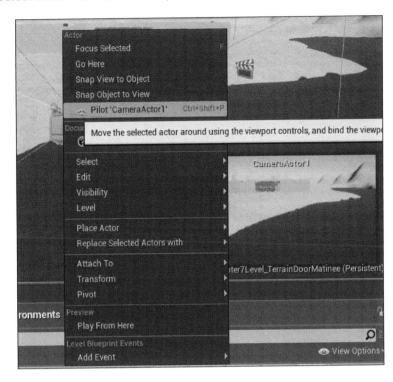

Move the viewport to the position you want to have the second keyframe in. This screenshot shows the position of the second keyframe camera:

When the viewport is positioned, as shown in the preceding screenshot, click on the icon in the top-left corner of the viewport to stop the pilot mode in order to fix the keyframe here. The location of the icon is shown here:

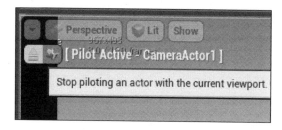

Following the shot plan we decided on, I have moved **Camera1** along the path up to the fireplace. To add the second camera, repeat the steps to create a new camera group and name the new camera as `Camera2`.

Now, move the first keyframe to the end of Camera1's final keyframe timeline. For me, this is set at **8.50s**; I moved the camera to the corner of the room, as shown in the following screenshot:

Repeat the steps to create keyframes for **Camera2**, move it along the path toward the running man, and then focus on the running man's face.

Now, we have two cameras that need to be told which one is playing at which part along the timeline. To do so, we need to create a new director group. The director group will dictate which camera is on air and what will be showing on screen. Go back to **Tracks** in the Matinee Editor. Right-click and select **Add New Director Group**, as shown in this screenshot:

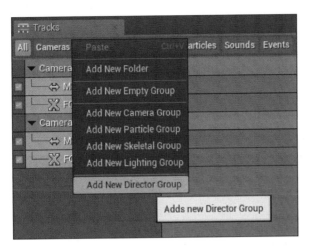

This creates a **Director** track above the camera tracks. Select the newly added **Director** track at 0.00, go to the ribbon at the top, and select **Add Key**, as shown in this screenshot:

The contextual menu will request that you select **Camera1** or **Camera2**. In this case, select **Camera1**. This fills up the entire duration of the cinematics. To create a key at 8.50s where **Camera1** and **Camera2** overlap, click on the **Director** track again and select **Add Key**. This time round, select **Camera2**. Move this key to **8.50**. This screenshot shows where the cameras are set up so that they can play correctly:

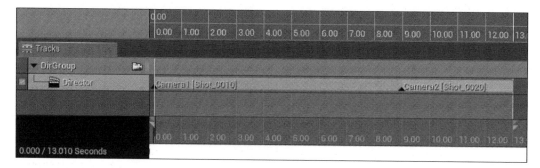

Finally, we are ready to play the cut scene. To tell the game to play the cut scene when starting the game, we need to use Blueprint. I hope you still remember how to use the Blueprint Editor. Click and open the Level Blueprint. Add the **Event BeginPlay** node and right-click and search for **Play**. Select the **Play Matineee Actor** option and link the nodes, as shown in the following screenshot. Now, save and play the level. You will see the entire matinee play before you control the player in the level.

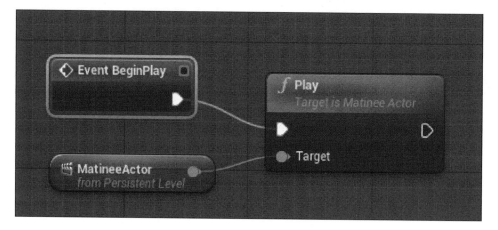

Summary

We covered terrain creation and matinee creation in this chapter. I hope you were able to enhance the game level with the new skills we explored.

Terrain manipulation covers large areas of a map; hence, we also went through the factors that affect the playability of the map. We also went through a simple exercise to create the outdoor terrain of our map with some hills and a lake.

Matinee creation involves a lot more technical planning before we start playing around with the editor itself. The use of the editor is pretty simple as it is similar to current video editors in the market. The techniques to create good cinematics were covered to help you understand their backgrounds a little better.

This is the last chapter of the book and the final summary. I sincerely hope that you enjoyed reading this book and had fun playing around with Unreal Engine 4. Lastly, I would like to wish you all the best in creating your own games. Do keep at it; there is always more to learn and other new tools out there to help you create what you want. I am sure that you love creating games; if not, you would not have survived this boring book right to the end. This book only serves to introduce you to the world of game development and shows you the basic tools to create a game using Unreal Engine. The rest of this journey is now left to you to create a game that is fun. Good luck! Don't forget to drop me a note to let me know about the games you create in the future. I am waiting to hear from you.

Index

Symbols

3D model
  animating 141
  preparing, for animation 141, 142
3ds Max
  animation, importing from 143

A

adjusted camera functions
  about 227
  Depth of field (DOF) 228, 229
  Field of view (FOV) 227, 228
  Zoom 227
AI
  implementing, in games 187
AIController
  configuring 175
  linking, to Character Blueprint 174
  movement speed, adjusting 177
AI logic
  basic animation, adding 175
  setting up 169, 170
Ambient Sound Actor 204
animation
  3D model, preparing for 141, 142
  about 140
  blending 147
  computer animation 140
  creating 142
  importing, from 3ds Max 143
  importing, from Maya 143
  stop-motion animation 140
Animation and Rigging Toolset (ART) 143

Animation Blueprint
  setting up, for Blend Animation
    usage 151-153
animation, in Unreal Engine 4 143
animation pack
  importing, from Marketplace 143-145
AnimGraph 154-157
**application programming
    interfaces (APIs) 115**
artificial intelligence (AI) 139, 162
audio, obtaining into Unreal
  about 201
  audio format 201
  bit depth 202
  sampling rate 201
  supported sound channels 202, 203
audio quality 200
Audio Volume 80

B

baking 67
beginners guide, Unreal Editor
  Content Browser 16
  Modes window 19
  Project Browser 16
  Scene Outliner 18
  start menu 15
  Toolbar 17
  Viewport 18
Behavior Tree
  about 163
  creating 179, 180
  custom task, creating for 182-185
  implementing, in Unreal Engine 4 167
  logic, designing of 164

Thank you for buying
Learning Unreal Engine
Game Development

About Packt Publishing

Packt, pronounced 'packed', published its first book, *Mastering phpMyAdmin for Effective MySQL Management*, in April 2004, and subsequently continued to specialize in publishing highly focused books on specific technologies and solutions.

Our books and publications share the experiences of your fellow IT professionals in adapting and customizing today's systems, applications, and frameworks. Our solution-based books give you the knowledge and power to customize the software and technologies you're using to get the job done. Packt books are more specific and less general than the IT books you have seen in the past. Our unique business model allows us to bring you more focused information, giving you more of what you need to know, and less of what you don't.

Packt is a modern yet unique publishing company that focuses on producing quality, cutting-edge books for communities of developers, administrators, and newbies alike. For more information, please visit our website at www.packtpub.com.

Writing for Packt

We welcome all inquiries from people who are interested in authoring. Book proposals should be sent to author@packtpub.com. If your book idea is still at an early stage and you would like to discuss it first before writing a formal book proposal, then please contact us; one of our commissioning editors will get in touch with you.

We're not just looking for published authors; if you have strong technical skills but no writing experience, our experienced editors can help you develop a writing career, or simply get some additional reward for your expertise.

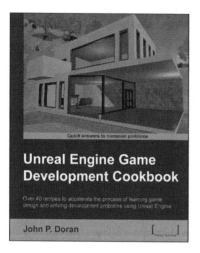

Unreal Engine Game Development Cookbook

ISBN: 978-1-78439-816-3   Paperback: 326 pages

Over 40 recipes to accelerate the process of learning game design and solving development problems using Unreal Engine

1. Explore the quickest way to tackle common challenges faced in Unreal Engine.

2. Create your own content, levels, light scenes, and materials, and work with Blueprints and C++ scripting.

3. An intermediate, fast-paced Unreal Engine guide with targeted recipes to design games within its framework.

Learning Unreal® Engine iOS Game Development

ISBN: 978-1-78439-771-5   Paperback: 212 pages

Create exciting iOS games with the power of the new Unreal® Engine 4 subsystems

1. Learn each step in the iOS game development process, from start to finish.

2. Develop exciting iOS games with the Unreal Engine 4.x toolset.

3. Step-by-step tutorials to build optimized iOS games.

Please check **www.PacktPub.com** for information on our titles

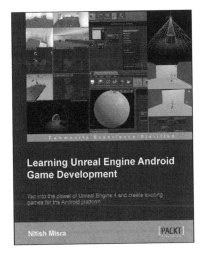

Learning Unreal Engine Android Game Development

ISBN: 978-1-78439-436-3   Paperback: 300 pages

Tap into the power of Unreal Engine 4 and create exciting games for the Android platform

1. Dive straight into making fully functional Android games with this hands-on guide.

2. Learn about the entire Android pipeline, from game creation to game submission.

3. Use Unreal Engine 4 to create a first-person puzzle game.

UnrealScript Game Programming Cookbook

ISBN: 978-1-84969-556-5   Paperback: 272 pages

Discover how you can augment your game development with the power of UnrealScript

1. Create a truly unique experience within UDK using a series of powerful recipes to augment your content.

2. Discover how you can utilize the advanced functionality offered by the Unreal Engine with UnrealScript.

3. Learn how to harness the built-in AI in UDK to its full potential.

Please check **www.PacktPub.com** for information on our titles

Made in the USA
Middletown, DE
11 June 2018